ON THE LYRICISM OF THE MIND

On the Lyricism of the Mind: Psychoanalysis and Literature explores the lyrical dimension (or the lyricism) of the psychic space. It is not presented as an artistic disposition, but rather as a universal psychic quality that enables the recovery and recuperation of the self. The specific nature of human lyricism is defined as the interaction as well as the integration of two psychic modes of experience, originally defined by the psychoanalyst Wilfred Bion: the emergent and the continuous principles of the self.

Dana Amir elaborates upon Bion's general notion of an interaction between the emergent and the continuous principles of the self, offering a discussion of the specific function of each principle and of the significance of the various types of interaction between them as the basis for mental health or pathology. The author applies these theoretical notions in her analytic work by means of literary illustrations, showing how the lyrical dimension may be used in analytical work as well as in psychoanalytic reading of literature and to explore the connection between psychoanalytic and literary languages.

On the Lyricism of the Mind presents a new psychoanalytic understanding of the capacity to heal, to grieve, to love and to know, using literary illustrations but also literary language in order to extract a new formulation out of the classic psychoanalytic language of Winnicott and Bion. This book will appeal to a wide audience including psychoanalysts, psychotherapists and art therapists. It is also extremely relevant to literary scholars, including students of literary criticism, philosophers of language and philosophers of mind, novelists, poets, and to a wide educated readership in general.

Dr Dana Amir is a clinical psychologist, supervising-analyst at the Israel Psychoanalytic Society, poetess and literature researcher, and a faculty member of Haifa University. She is the author of five poetry books and two psychoanalytic non-fiction books, and the winner of the Adler National Poetry Prize (1993); the Bahat Prize for Academic Original Book (2006); the Frances Tustin International Memorial Prize (2011); the Prime Minister's Prize for Hebrew Writers (2012); the IPA (International Psychoanalytic Association) Sacerdoti Prize (2013); the Nathan Alterman Poetry Prize (2013) and the Distinguished Psychoanalytic Educators Award (IFPE).

PSYCHOANALYSIS IN A NEW KEY BOOK SERIES
DONNEL STERN
Series Editor

When music is played in a new key, the melody does not change, but the notes that make up the composition do: change in the context of continuity, continuity that perseveres through change. Psychoanalysis in a New Key publishes books that share the aims psychoanalysts have always had, but that approach them differently. The books in the series are not expected to advance any particular theoretical agenda, although to this date most have been written by analysts from the Interpersonal and Relational orientations.

The most important contribution of a psychoanalytic book is the communication of something that nudges the reader's grasp of clinical theory and practice in an unexpected direction. Psychoanalysis in a New Key creates a deliberate focus on innovative and unsettling clinical thinking. Because that kind of thinking is encouraged by exploration of the sometimes surprising contributions to psychoanalysis of ideas and findings from other fields, Psychoanalysis in a New Key particularly encourages interdisciplinary studies. Books in the series have married psychoanalysis with dissociation, trauma theory, sociology, and criminology. The series is open to the consideration of studies examining the relationship between psychoanalysis and any other field – for instance, biology, literary and art criticism, philosophy, systems theory, anthropology, and political theory.

But innovation also takes place within the boundaries of psychoanalysis, and Psychoanalysis in a New Key therefore also presents work that reformulates thought and practice without leaving the precincts of the field. Books in the series focus, for example, on the significance of personal values in psychoanalytic practice, on the complex interrelationship between the analyst's clinical work and personal life, on the consequences for the clinical situation when patient and analyst are from different cultures, and on the need for psychoanalysts to accept the degree to which they knowingly satisfy their own wishes during treatment hours, often to the patient's detriment.

ON THE LYRICISM
OF THE MIND

Psychoanalysis and literature

Dana Amir

Routledge
Taylor & Francis Group

LONDON AND NEW YORK

First published in English as *On the Lyricism of the Mind: Psychoanalysis and literature* 2016
by Routledge
2 Park Square, Milton Park, Abingdon, Oxon, OX14 4RN

and by Routledge
711 Third Avenue, New York, NY 10017

Routledge is an imprint of the Taylor & Francis Group, an informa business

This book is a translation of a work previously published in Hebrew as *Al Haliriyut Shel Ha-Nefesh* by Haifa University Press and the Hebrew University Press (Magness).

Translation into English by Mirjam Hadar.

Trademark notice: Product or corporate names may be trademarks or registered trademarks, and are used only for identification and explanation without intent to infringe.

British Library Cataloguing in Publication Data
A catalogue record for this book is available from the British Library

Library of Congress Cataloging in Publication Data
Amir, Dana.
['Al ha-liriyut shel ha-nefesh. English]
On the lyricism of the mind : psychoanalysis and literature / Dana Amir.
pages cm
Includes bibliographical references and index.
1. Self. 2. Psychology and literature. I. Title.
BF697.A49513 2016
155.2—dc23
2015025483

ISBN: 978-1-138-84178-9 (hbk)
ISBN: 978-1-138-84179-6 (pbk)
ISBN: 978-1-315-73197-1 (ebk)

Typeset in Bembo
by Swales & Willis Ltd, Exeter, Devon, UK
Printed and bound in Great Britain by
Ashford Colour Press Ltd, Gosport, Hampshire

In memory of my mother

CONTENTS

ACKNOWLEDGEMENTS

My deepest thanks go to a few people whose contribution to the English edition of this book will always be treasured:

To Donnel Stern, the Editor of the Psychoanalysis in a New Key series, who opened the door for this book warmly and generously, and whose psychoanalytic work is one of the most creative and inspiring illustrations of the idea of playing "in a new key" in order to make real music.

To Golan Shahar, whose unique work is a wonderful integration of science and art.

To Orit Sherry, whose deep wisdom and everlasting support has accompanied my writing for years, since its very first step.

To Michal, my one and true inspiration.

To my father and brothers, my soul mates, my rocks.

To my beloved children.

PROLOGUE

Many years ago, my father introduced me to an ancient Japanese poem:

> The deer on pine mountain,
> Where there are no falling leaves,
> Knows the coming of autumn
> Only by the sound of his own voice.
>
> (Ōnakatomi No Yoshinobu, tenth century)

I was maybe eight years old and probably understood very little of this. However, I remember the magic of the short lines, the curiosity that the enigmatic words arose in me, and most of all – the sense of vast space suddenly opened wild through the minimal description: a pine mountain, the coming autumn, a lonely deer. This poem stayed with me for many years. Today I can say that it touched upon one of the most fundamental questions that have occupied me ever since: the question of the relationship between internal and external, between what the human consciousness experiences as imposed from the outside – and what it experiences as created from within.

The deer on the pine mountain is not responsive to the outside – as it doesn't mark the change of seasons – but to his own voice, as if informed of the change only from within. But his voice does not echo only the autumn within but also the autumn outside, even if it is still concealed. This cross-section between what is transferred from within and what is transferred from without – between the consciousness that reads the external and the consciousness that writes this same external as if it were created from within – is in many ways the subject of this book.

What motivated the writing of it was my fascination with a psychic dimension of whose existence I have always been aware. It is not the psychic quality that generates poetry; rather, it is a dimension that not only resides in every psyche, but also is basically formative of psychic existence as it is. Rather than the poet's genius for reflecting on his own existence, it is the lyrical dimension of every human being as such, which makes existence possible.

As a poet, I was asked many times about how my psychoanalytic knowledge may influence my poetic writing. The truth is that one of the most precious things that poetry has taught me, in this context, concerns exactly the elusiveness of knowing. I am not pointing at the philosophical attitude claiming that there is no possibility of "really" knowing anything as such – but rather at the feeling that the same thing can be known and re-known in many ways, time and again. In that sense, practising psychoanalysis has no more influence on writing poetry than expertize in the chemical structure of water has on the capacity to enjoy the sound of waves at dawn.

And yet, how can the human psyche know and not know at the same time? What is the meaning of this cross-section between the permanent and the ever-changing, between the familiar and the alien, at any given moment?

These questions occupied, albeit in different ways, two main psychoanalytic thinkers. The first of these was Wilfred Bion, who described the human psyche as constituted by an emergent and continuous principle, emphasizing the way in which their varied interaction is responsible for humans' ability to tolerate change and development. The second was D.W.Winnicott, whose writings were dedicated to how human subjectivity arises in a potential space, within which inside and outside engage in a continuous dialectic.

This book actually brings together these two thinkers by describing the creation of the potential space from a Bionian vantage point, namely in terms of the interaction between the emergent and the continuous principle of the self. It is the interaction between these two principles that institutes what I call "the lyrical dimension of the potential space" and, in fact, the psyche itself qua space.

What are the emergent self and the continuous self?

The emergent self – or the emergent principle of the self – is the substrate that perceives the world, and the self within it, as being in constant flux, as inaccessible to common rules of interpretation and as unpredictable. If we were able to capture reality as it is observed through the prism of the emergent self, we would find ourselves facing something not merely capricious and singular, but also ungraspable and hence indefinable. Reality, as captured by the emergent self, cannot in fact be captured at all, as it is in constant emergence. The continuous self, by contrast, is the principle responsible for the perception of the world as continuous, predictable and open to explanation in terms of causality, time and space.

At no point in time should these two modes of being – the emergent and the continuous – be seen in isolation from one another. They do not lead a simply parallel existence in the psyche: they interact – and it is exactly this interaction that interests me the most, since its nature and quality determine the degree of their integration, hence also the nature and quality of the lyrical dimension. The more constructive the interaction, the greater an extent of integration between the emergent and the continuous facets becomes possible, and the greater the degree of this integration, the higher the quality of the lyrical dimension.

What, then, is the lyrical dimension of the psyche?

The lyrical dimension of the psyche is the dimension that transforms the psyche from being a plane, determined by one emergent axis and one continuous axis of experience, into a space that integrates these two. In fact, the very sense of interiority yielded by this integration is tantamount to the sense of selfhood: our experience of ourselves as having boundaries, depth and meaning. The lyrical dimension is the psychic dimension that enables us to create a narrative out of the mere facts of our lives – not only to undergo and bear the experience but also to store it as a memory; as an experiential continuum including both outline and depth, stability and movement, support relying on reality testing and support based on the ability to perceive the singular quality and uniqueness of things.

Why *lyrical* and not *poetic*?

As I see it, the lyrical actually combines the poetic and the prosaic. The poetic element of language infuses each common word with private and singular meaning. The prosaic element of language, by contrast, uses words in their shared meanings and thereby allows for dialogue. Every dialogue contains varying proportions of poetic and prosaic elements, depending on the type of relationship between the participants, on the degree of intimacy of the situation and on circumstantial factors. If the language of the emergent self is poetic, and the language of the continuous self is prosaic, then the lyrical is the psychic "idiolect" in which these two languages intersect; it is what captures every experience from both its most singular, ineffable and inexplicable side as well as its general and common one.

In other words, the continuous self is responsible for the spatial outlines of the psyche, while the emergent self is in charge of the constant motion between them. The emergent self is responsible for internalizing the world as a unique, inexplicable and constantly changing phenomenon, while the continuous self controls the internalization of the world as a common, stable phenomenon that can be rendered conceptually and is discursively accessible. It is the intersection between these two modes of existence, or states of aggregation, that enables the psyche to experience the fullness of itself, as well as the fullness of the world.

My examination of the notion of the lyrical dimension starts with a discussion of Bion and Winnicott's relevant notions. It continues with an investigation of the philosophical and human meaning of the lyrical dimension. Subsequently, I describe the interrelations between the emergent and the continuous principles within the primary dyad, as well as the pathological meaning of damage to the integration between emergent and continuous principles with regard both to this primary dyad and to the developing self. I will further discuss the notions of *actual self* and *potential self* (based on Gilead's solution to the mind-body question) and their interrelations as originating from the interaction between the continuous self and the emergent self. To conclude, I will consider the relevance of the notion of the lyrical dimension to the three most important capacities of the human psyche: the ability to mourn, the ability to know and the ability to love.

Throughout the chapters, I refer not only to a variety of psychoanalytic thinkers but also to a variety of illustrations taken from literary prose and poetry. This choice is connected not only to my love for literature, both as a reader and a writer, but also to my belief that it is literature that represents, more than any other expression, the power of human lyricism.

To return to the poem with which I opened this prologue – we can think of the deer as analogous to a poet, and of his capacity to anticipate the coming of autumn by the sound of his own voice as analogous to his use of the lyrical; holding steadily enough his voice's continuous aspect in order to be able to contain the change that emerges in it with the coming of fall, and to extract meaning from it.

1

BION, WINNICOTT AND THE LYRICAL DIMENSION OF THE POTENTIAL SPACE

The question concerning the foundations of psychic movement and psychic change is probably the very basis for every attempt to define the human experience. Two theoretical approaches touch on this issue, attempting to define mental dynamics in terms of the interaction between two aspects of the self: one is D.W. Winnicott's theoretical viewpoint, which casts light on the complex dialectic between inside and outside, and the other is Wilfred Bion's perspective, which clarifies the relations of containment between an emergent aspect and a continuous aspect of the personality as a whole.

Winnicott and the playground of the potential space

Winnicott argues that at the start of an infant's life, mother and infant constitute a new psychological entity that exceeds the mere sum of its parts, much like an interaction between two mutually responsive components that yield a kind of compound or overlap. Where this overlap occurs, an aspect of the mother merges with the infant to create a state that Winnicott (1951) calls *primary maternal preoccupation*, where the self is lost in the other. This does not refer to the infant's experience, as he or she doesn't own a self that can be lost at this stage. It refers to the mother's part in the mother–infant dyad, a part that constitutes a continuum whose respective end points are pathological: while in one pole there is no aspect of the mother that is available to unite with the infant – the other pole is demonstrated by the mother of whom no aspect exists outside the experience of primary maternal preoccupation. A mother who finds herself in the first pole experiences her baby as an alien, perhaps even an attacking object. A mother who finds herself in the second pole, on the other hand, uses the mother–infant unit as a type of psychotic shelter: her fusion with her baby comes at the expense of her sense of reality and of the experience that she exists at all in a reality beyond that of the mother–infant unit.

Where maternal preoccupation is undamaged, the illusion of a *subjective object* is provided by the mother: the illusion that inner and outer realities are one and the same. In fact, the mother "suspends" the infant's consciousness of separateness by responding to his or her needs before they escalate into a desire.

Winnicott (1945, 1971a) repeatedly emphasizes that at the beginning of the child's life the mother must be responsive to him or her in this way in order to avoid a premature consciousness of separateness. Yet at the same time, mothering must not be too perfect. Once each and every one of the infant's needs is anticipated and met, even before he or she has experienced the need as such, the essential experience of desire becomes well nigh impossible (Winnicott, 1954–1955, p. 268). Paradoxically – and Winnicott's writings are not only replete with paradoxes, but also identify them as a necessary feature of the human experience – while the mother must shield the infant from premature consciousness of desire and separateness, she must at the same time allow the infant the opportunity to experience desire along with its concomitant sense of separateness.

Whether the infant will be able to make use of the experience of impulse depends on the extent to which the mother has succeeded to suspend – yet also to preserve – the infant's consciousness of desire until he or she reaches the point at which they can experience feelings as their own. Before this time, the infant is likely to experience any impulse as an external attack; an experience that might damage his or her self-generated desire. The instincts can be experienced as much externally as can a clap of thunder or a hit, claims Winnicott: "The infant's ego is building up strength and in consequence is getting towards a state in which id-demands will be felt as part of the self, and not as environmental" (Winnicott, 1960, p. 141). Once a clearer sense of self begins to emerge, the experience of impulse serves to organize and focus the infant's feeling of him or herself as the authentic creator of his or her experience. The infant's being is formed as he or she learns to feel their desires and act upon them (Winnicott, 1967). When there is an ongoing and severe failure in providing a good enough holding environment, the infant is hurled into a chaotic state in which he or she experiences a disturbed sense of continued existence, namely of his or her "going on being" (Winnicott, 1963, p. 183).

When this dysfunction of the holding environment is less severe, the infant may develop a defensive personality structure, constituted by transferring the function of protection and caring from the mother to him or herself. Winnicott (1960) calls this personality structure, which evolves under a sense of danger, the *false self*. In this kind of organization, what develops instead of the rich mutual relationships resulting from the differentiation between the conscious and the unconscious and the emergence of a semi-penetrable repression barrier allowing a partial trickle of unconscious material to pass from the unconscious into consciousness – is a complete or partial alienation between one aspect of the self and another. The false self comes into being in order to ensure the defensive isolation of the true self (which enfolds the infantile potential of psychological individuality). But this isolation of the true self inevitably leads to a sense of emptiness, barrenness, uselessness and death. This raising of a wall around the self runs counter to the double and vital function of the unconscious in the course of normal development. On the one hand, such a function includes the censoring of charged contents and, on the other, their camouflaged and selective diffusion into consciousness. While the intact defense system allows not merely for organizing and denying the experience, but also for preserving the denied desire in the unconscious, the personality structure of the false self does not enable the development of the singular aspects of the self.

In the course of the development of *the capacity to be alone* (as opposed to being lonely), the infant's capacity to create the space in which he or she lives (the *potential space*) matures as well (Winnicott, 1958). This is an extremely personal space; one that is not circumscribed by the body, without being quite identical to what we experience as the psyche. In fact, this is the space within which we create, dream and play. It evolves under a paradoxical condition: the child must be allowed to play alone in the presence of the absent mother and in the absence of the present mother. What Winnicott meant by this paradoxical formulation was that the mother is not present in this stage as an object, but as an environment, or as the holding space in which the child is at play. Most notably, this environmental space is imperceptible as long as it is actually there. At this point, if the mother overemphasizes her presence, she causes her child to become addicted to her as an omnipotent object. As the child's capacity to be alone develops, the mother's role as the additional creator of the potential space (up to that point) passes to the child himself (Ogden, 1986).

Michael Balint (1968) compared the relation of the infant to the environmental-mother with the adult's attitude to air: it is only when we are deprived of air that we realize how shockingly total our dependence upon it is. Accordingly, when the relations with the environment-mother collapse, this brings about a terrifying realization of the child's dependence upon the mother who is absent as an object. When this happens, the infant develops a defensive, artificial separateness and mobilizes all his or her powers to mature as soon as possible, so as to anticipate the threat from a less vulnerable position. Falling asleep, as well as the ability to dream, are both connected with our ability to rely safely upon the internalized environmental-mother, since they are associated with our ability to trust that we shall continue to exist even when we surrender our conscious control.

At this early developmental stage of the transitional phenomenon, the infant should not be suddenly confronted with the fact that he or she has a psyche of their own. They must be given respite so as to discover this by themselves. What enables the infant to become weaned from the mother's psychological support is the very existence of the paradox: the mother and the infant are one and simultaneously two. The baby created the object that was there to be discovered. According to Winnicott (1951), the baby should never be asked whether he or she created the object or found it. Both possibilities are equally true. Maintaining the emotional truth of union with the mother along with that of separateness from her is what allows for play within the potential space.

There is an essential difference between the experience of absence of the mother as an object and the experience of absence of the environment-mother. The former experience characterizes the phase during which relation to the mother as a whole object emerges (this phase, in a sense, is identical to the depressive phase, as Melanie Klein [1935, 1940] defined it). Hence, while the reaction to losing the mother as an object may involve grief, loneliness and guilt; since the ability to be alone has already been attained – i.e. the environment-mother has been internalized – the infant can cope with this loss. The loss of the environment-mother, by contrast, is a catastrophic event attended by a sense that the infant himself is in a severe danger of being lost. Here the infant feels on the verge of total evaporation. At stake is not how the infant exists but whether he or she exists at all. This is why patients who are in a parallel condition to the above infantile state may develop autistic regression as a way of coping with the sense of psychic catastrophe.

During the period of whole-object relatedness, the infant is not engaged in the subjective creation of the mother, but in discovering her as an external presence. His or her continued emotional development, including the ability for object usage (Winnicott, 1969), depends on the mother's ability to survive over time as such an external object. The fact that the infant destroys the object (in phantasy) while the maternal object survives this destruction is what makes it possible for him or her to discover the object's external nature (Winnicott, 1969). Objectively seen, the external mother has been there all along and it is she who, together with the infant, created the illusion of the subjective object. But it is exactly because this illusion was created and successfully maintained that the infant could remain unconscious of the mother's external existence. This is probably the crux of the Winnicottian paradox: the infant met the mother, but did not perceive her as a separate object. He saw the mother as his or her own creation. The process of giving up the internal object (which is under the infant's ultimate control) in favour of an external one (which exists outside of such a control) is not obvious. To a great extent it is an expression of trust, since it depends on the external object's readiness to be there for the child:

> From now on the subject says: "Hello object!" "I destroyed you." "I love you." "You have value for me because of your survival of my destruction of you." "While I am loving you I am all the time destroying you in (unconscious) fantasy." Here fantasy begins for the individual. The subject can now use the object that has survived.
>
> *(Winnicott, 1971b, pp. 89–90)*

So far, he or she was unable to grasp the real qualities of the object, or the fact that the object is rooted in a world outside the self. This is also why he or she could not use the object. In fact, the illusion of the subjective object puts in abeyance the discovery of the world of objects – namely the discovery of the people with whom the infant will be able to share experiences in the outside world. The object's persistence is expressed in the mother's presence as an external object over time, while the infant tries to release his or her grip on the mother as an internal object.

What are the conditions for a situation of an inability to release the internal object? Such a situation arises when the mother, as an external object, fails to be there when the infant allows him or herself to surrender to her, or when the infant's experience with the illusion of the subjective object has not evoked the trust that he or she needs to be able to surrender to the external object. Once the survival of the external object fails (when it provides neither the physical nor the psychological presence that the infant needs), the infant will tighten his or her grip on the omnipotent internal object, which thus becomes his or her one safe haven. Imprisoning him or herself in the magical inner world of objects, and rigidly clinging to it, the infant evolves an extremely limited ability to either identify or use the external world of objects.

In the process of discovering the external nature of objects, the infant is also led to recognize his or her own influence on the external mother–object that has just been revealed. So far, the child has been treating his mother with a degree of selfish cruelty, namely without compassion or care (Winnicott, 1954–1955). This is not the result of an omnipotent urge to hurt her, but because the infant has not yet developed an awareness to the object as a subject, and hence has no empathy towards it. On discovery of the externality of objects, the infant feels the cruelty that accompanies his or her using them to satisfy needs, thus develops an unconscious fear that this demandingness may damage them. The maternal function during this period is to maintain the situation over time (Winnicott, 1954–1955; 1969) so that while in the infant's unconscious phantasy he or she hurts the mother – it becomes obvious that the mother is alive and present independently. This simultaneous experience of the destruction of the internal mother-object and of the ongoing relations with the mother as an external object that is not vengeful is what affords the infant two forms of further experience: internal and external. The distinction between internal and external reality is not the result of one instant act, but rather of a dynamic process in which the internal object must be incessantly destroyed in the unconscious phantasy, so as to again and again make space for discovering the external one.

Winnicott speaks of three types of infantile dependence: in the earliest developmental stage, the infant can survive and develop only under the protective and suspending wrap of a holding maternal environment. During this phase, the mother supplies the illusion of a subjective object (the illusion that internal and external reality are identical), thereby protecting the infant from knowing about his or her separateness. When the transitional phenomenon sets in, the developmental task of the mother–infant dyad becomes the infant's non-traumatic weaning from the maternal supplement. This is achieved in part when the infant plays alone in the presence of the absent mother and in the absence of the present mother – or perhaps in the presence of the environment-mother and in the absence of the mother as an object. An over-intervention of the mother in the infant's play, in this phase, will lead to extreme dependence on the real external mother. The third type of dependence is the infant's reliance on the mother's ability to survive over time during the period of whole-object relatedness. Until this point, the world of internal objects overshadowed that of external ones. Now, the infant undergoes a process of renouncing the internal mother-object, thereby making space for the discovery of the real mother. In contrast with the object that was allegedly "created" by the infant, the now revealed external object turns out to be open to a totally different usage, since the relations with it are grounded in a world that is beyond the child's omnipotent control.

Though the potential space arises from the physical and psychological space between mother and child, an unimpaired course of development allows each individual the opportunity to create his or her own potential space. The ability to do so is based on a set of psychic moves and their dialectic relations. Winnicott (1971a) describes the transitional space as the hypothetical field which may (or may not) come into existence between infant and object (the mother or part of the mother), by the end of the period marked by the infant's merging with the object. Elsewhere he refers to the transitional space as a middle area of experience situated between internal and external reality. This, in fact, may be understood as the space spread between the subjective object and the objectively perceived object, between "me-extensions" and "not-me", between our own existing as objects and our existing as subjects.

In his book *The Matrix of the Mind* (1986), Thomas Ogden relates to human subjectivity in terms of the ability to maintain several levels of self-consciousness, starting from intentional self-observation (a very late achievement) and ending with the most subtle sense of "being myself" – where experience is suffused with a faint quality of "I am the one who thinks my thoughts and feels my feelings", in contrast with a form of reflex-like responsiveness. While subjectivity is connected with consciousness, Ogden argues, it is not identical to it. The experience of consciousness results from having achieved subjectivity. No consciousness, that is, can exist without subjectivity and it is doubtful whether subjectivity is possible in the total absence of consciousness (Ogden, 1986).

The very focus of Winnicott's work on the notion of the potential space is formed by the developmental stage during which the earliest awareness of separateness emerges. To prevent a traumatic transition from the mother–infant dyad to the stage in which mother and infant each exist in their own right, Winnicott suggested the existence of a potential space that is located between mother and infant. This space is always potential (and never real) as it contains the paradox of union-separateness; a paradox that, according to Winnicott, cannot be resolved. The transition from the experience of the environment-mother to the perception of the mother as separate object requires an ability to shift between states of union and separateness. In this context, Winnicott (1958) points at the transitional object as the symbol of separateness within union, as well as of union within separateness, since it is an omnipotent extension of the infant itself, while at the same time being an object that exists outside the child's control:

> I should like to put in a reminder here that the essential feature in the concept
> of transitional objects and phenomena (according to my presentation of the
> subject) is the paradox, and the acceptance of the paradox: the baby creates
> the object, but the object was there waiting to be created and to become
> a cathected object. I tried to draw attention to this aspect of transitional
> phenomena by claiming that in the rules of the game we all know that we
> will never challenge the baby to elicit an answer to the question: did you
> create that or did you find it?
>
> *(Winnicott, 1971b, p. 89)*

At the very point at which the world provided the infant with the object, the
infant created it. Hence the transitional object is neither "me" nor "not-me". It is
charged with meaning bestowed by the mother, but it is not itself the mother; it is
charged with meaning given by the self, yet it is not the self. While the transitional
object reflects the self as mother it also reflects the mother as self, and it can never
be reduced to just one of these options. The developmental significance of the
transitional object is that through it the infant makes the transition from the stage
in which the object is perceived as an object constituted by the infantile subject –
to one in which it is perceived as an external object that exists outside the infantile
omnipotent control. Being the first "not-I" object, the transitional object allows
the baby to shift back and forth between subjectivity and objectivity, between
symbiosis and separateness. With the passing of time, the transitional object
becomes less emotionally charged. It is not merely forgotten, nor is it mourned;
rather it simply loses its meaning, since the nature of transitional phenomena is to
become diffuse. In fact, they become extended over the whole intermediate space
between internal reality and the outside world (Kulka, 1995).

The Winnicottian psyche is a huge playground. The game of hide-and-seek –
Winnicott's well-known metaphor for the dialectic that forms the very foundation
of human existence – consists of the eternal integration between the wish for being
discovered and the wish not to be found; between the wish to leave the deepest
concealed secret of our existence out of sight and the wish to be known and
understood, to belong and be seen.

There are two types of people, I was once told, who are not able to enjoy
theatre: those who constantly remember that it is only a performance – and those
who believe that the actions on stage are not a performance at all. While the first
watch the show from an excessive distance, the second have no sense of distance
whatsoever. While the first pay the price of alienation, the second pay the price of
anxiety. Neither case allows for an area of play. Enjoying theatre (and this includes
all sorts of theatre, including the theatres of life) requires the ability to know that
at the end of the show the curtain will fall – yet to believe that what we see is
far from being merely an act. Our ability to play relies on our knowing that we
are at play – while believing wholeheartedly, nevertheless, that this play is reality
itself. All areas of creativity, work and love are grounded on this dialectic between
knowing the reality outside us and feeling that we have the ability to create this
reality, according to our wishes, each and every moment.

Wilfred Bion and the relationship between container and contained

In the second half of the twentieth century, Wilfred Bion started to publish his original ideas about the relationship between container and contained and its key role in psychological development. Though his ideas referred to the work of Melanie Klein, he succeeded to call attention to a new angle on the processes of psychological development, as well as the therapeutic process. According to Bion (1962a), the human personality consists of two components – container and contained. What he meant was not a static construct but rather a dynamic situation characterized by a contained seeking a container (and vice versa) through a dynamic interaction. This container/contained relationship can be identified throughout the human psyche and plays a main and critical role in mental development. The contained and the container give rise to an interactive system: the container may be so rigid that it crushes its content (the contained), sterilizes it and robs it of its features. Alternatively, the content (the contained) might fill the container to bursting, pushing it beyond its breaking point. When there are especially high levels of hostility between container and contained the result is mutual destruction. When, on the contrary, the relationship is based on love, the two will enable each other's growth.

The model from which Bion deduced his conceptual principles is one of mother–infant relations where the mother serves as a container for the infant, so that both will have the opportunity to grow due to the experience of containing and containment. Bion generalized the principles of this inter-personal interaction to all existing forms of interaction, including various forms of intra-psychic interaction. Moreover, Bion argued that these two components underlie not just the personality structure but also the process of thinking. He believed that there is a hierarchy starting with low-level or embryonic thoughts, which progress developmentally to a high, pure and non-concrete abstract level of thought. The very bottom of the scale is formed by elements that are neither psychic nor material, but rather a composition of the two. He called the latter *beta elements*. These are basic elements that undergo a kind of "purification" and become more abstract through the stages of development. The process is a gradual one, within which the movement from one level to the next is driven by a container (in effect, a pre-conception) that is in search of a contained (an actualization). The mating between container and contained results in a conception. In the next stage this conception transforms into a pre-conception that is looking for a new actualization, thus starting the cycle again. And so the evolution of thought from a low level to a higher level of complexity occurs according to a model whereby the container/contained operate in an environment that stimulates growth. It is, in other words, the quality of the container/contained interaction that allows the mutual flourishing of the two elements, and this is what allows for emotional experience to be held and contained within the psyche.

The interaction between container/contained may take one of three forms: parasitic, symbiotic or commensal. The link is considered parasitic when the object created by the container/contained interaction destroys both container and contained; it is regarded as symbiotic when it eventually issues in the development of powers of expression, and it is regarded commensal when the feelings involved serve to develop the individual's capacity to invent new forms of language that support emotional development (Symington and Symington, 1996, p. 56).

Like Freud, Bion assumed that the psyche includes a kind of *contact barrier*,[1] which, under normal circumstances, prevents elements belonging to one state of mind from interfering with those belonging to another. Such a barrier separates conscious mental phenomena from unconscious ones. Its partial permeability allows a degree of interchange between the two areas while avoiding the flooding of one by the other. Storage in memory and repression, too, are made possible by the existence of this barrier. Normally, the human subject is not bombarded with unconscious material while engaging in a conversation (something that would certainly prevent normal communication). Meanwhile, however, it allows enough unconscious phantasy to percolate through to consciousness, thus rendering the conversation with depth and resonance. Without this, the interchange would stay rigid and sterile. When, on the other hand, there is an excess of flooding, the exchange might become psychotic. Bion assumed that the same barrier also exists between what he called *beta elements* (perceptual input) and *alpha elements* (primitive thoughts). The attempt to understand how the individual passes from the non-thought area of beta-elements to the area of alpha elements caused Bion to postulate the existence of a container/contained mechanism, where beta elements are the contained.

This is how he defined the concepts of container and contained in his "Learning from Experience":

> Melanie Klein has described an aspect of projective identification concerned with the modification of infantile fears; the infant projects a part of its psyche, namely its bad feelings, into a good breast. Thence in due course they are removed and re-introjected. During their sojourn in the good breast they are felt to have been modified in such a way that the object that is re-introjected has become tolerable to the infant's psyche. From the above theory I shall abstract for use as a model the idea of a container into which an object is projected and the object that can be projected into the container: the latter I shall designate by the term contained.
>
> *(Bion, 1962b, p. 89)*

Within the mother–infant dyad, the mother processes the infant's unbearable primitive sensations (beta elements), which the infant projects into the mother by means of her own *alpha function*. The process depends on the mother's ability to take in the emotionally intolerable experience, to tolerate and process it and to return it to the infant in an ameliorated, bearable form. The mother's attitude of mind while doing so is called *reverie*, and a central factor determining the quality of her alpha function is her love. It is through the mother's interaction with the infant that the latter internalizes a knowing and knowledge-imparting object. An individual who internalizes such an object will be capable of self-knowledge and of communication among different aspects of him or herself, as well as becoming capable of reflection. But when an infant perceives the mother as hostile to his or her attempts at projective identification, this gives him or her a sense of a world that wishes neither to know nor to be known. For such an infant, any form of integration will constitute an insufferable threat. Thus, the container/contained model of mother–infant relations is internalized in the infant's psyche as an interactive mould into which, at a later stage, emotional and perceptual contents are poured. This mould will become one's cognitive scheme, namely one's mode of coping with perceptual and emotional data to the point of experiencing oneself as a psychological subject.

In the course of his work with psychotic patients, Bion learned that the psychotic person – or the psychotic component in every personality – is unable to suffer the psychic reality. This is why the psychotic individual resists thinking. Under normal conditions, the individual holds experiences in his or her mind long enough to allow alpha function to become operative and mitigate them. The process of thinking provides a degree of containment for painful experiences, and thus makes them more tolerable. The psychotic person, in contrast, is unable to suffer frustration or moderate it by means of thought, and therefore manages the psychic stress by evacuating it through the muscular system. What is evacuated is the unthinkable emotional experience or, in other words, beta elements that cannot be transformed through the psyche's alpha function. The psychotic subject evacuates his or her psyche while remaining trapped within oneself without the escape route offered by thinking, and so stays in a state of gradual starvation. Threatened by the persecutory feelings that accompany it, the psychotic subject tries to annihilate consciousness. Any process of integration arouses great resistance, since it may put the fragments back together into one entity and thus force him or her to deal with a cruel and terrorizing super-ego. Thus Bion observed a mental process that fails to occur in the psychotic part of the personality and whose absence or destruction cause psychotic patients to manifest severe impairment of the ability to pay attention, to remember, to judge and to generate visual-associative images. He understood that the psychotic patient actively attacks these psychic functions in order to avoid integration, therefore barring oneself from the input necessary for psychic development.

In an unpublished paper entitled "Catastrophic Change" (1967) – later reprinted as "Container and Contained Transformed" (in *Attention and Interpretation*, 1970) – Bion touched upon two key principles at work in the human psyche. The first of these two, the *emergent principle*, perceives the world as undergoing a constant change. The second, the *continuous principle*, perceives the world as stable and fixed. In this paper, which describes the interaction between what Bion defines as "the Establishment" (representing the stable, sometimes rigid force that resists change) and "the messianic idea" (which represents the force of innovation and change), he argues that the aspect of the personality that always stays stable and fixed is actually the only force that can contain new perceptions of the self and of the world:

The individual always displays some aspect of his personality that is stable and constant even though it may sometimes be very difficult to detect in the welter of evidence for instability; it may appear only in the regularity with which the patient attends his sessions. In this stability will be found the counterpart of what [...] I have called the Establishment. It will be maintained with great tenacity as the only force likely to contain the counterpart of the messianic idea. Reciprocally, the messianic idea is the only force likely to withstand the pressures of the counterpart of the Establishment in the individual.

(Bion, 1970, p. 121)[2]

If the interaction between the emergent principle and the continuous principle of the self is mutually reinforcing, development will occur and change will be possible. If, by contrast, every change is experienced as a threat to the continuous identity – namely to the "continuous self" – any psychological change will be felt as catastrophic since it will be associated with the destruction of one's sense of continuity. When the continuous container cannot hold the emergent contained, the subjective experience is one of breakdown. In such circumstances, in order to maintain a sense of existential continuity, the psyche must resist all change and avoid the emergence of any new experience.

Bion himself never expanded on the unique significance of each of these elements of the self, and actually never dealt with them separately, but rather encompassed them in his general argument concerning the interaction between container and contained. The next chapters, therefore, offer ideas that come to elaborate Bion's general notion of an interaction between the emergent and the continuous principles of the self, offering a discussion of the specific function of each principle, as well as the significance of the various types of interaction between them as the basis for mental functioning or pathology.

This notion of an interaction between the emergent and the continuous will be elaborated by means of a discussion of Winnicott's potential space and the possible contribution of the interaction between the continuous self and the emergent self to its formation.

What are the main differences between Winnicott's and Bion's conceptions of the psychological space?

Winnicott's starting point, considering the constitution of the potential space, is the interaction between mother and infant. It is this interaction that announces the inauguration of the dialectic relations between internal and external reality. Bion, by contrast, stresses the importance of the constructive interaction between what is continuous and emergent within the self, and the ability of this self to tolerate growth and change. These relations are not merely the result of the interaction between the infant (the contained) and the mother (the container), but also the fruit of an inborn dynamic, so that they affect external reality no less than they are affected by it.

Winnicott's attitude to reality was, primarily, as to "a constant" which, hence, is essentially opposed to the ever-changing internal reality. Bion, too, underlines the role of the "constant" or "continuous" element within the psyche, but he does not locate this constant in the external reality: rather it is situated in a certain aspect of the self which experiences both itself and the world as continuous. This aspect, then, is contrasted with another part of the self that experiences itself as well as the world as incessantly changing.

Winnicott regards the ability to evolve subjective experience as a developmental achievement that relies on the ability to maintain dialectic between inside and outside, and between fantasy and reality. This achievement, therefore, depends on the infant's interaction with his mother in the earliest stages of life, and on his or her ability to withdraw from the symbiotic union with the mother in a non-traumatic way. Even though human beings experience this dialectic between inside and outside throughout the course of their lifetime, the formation of a potential space, which is both a condition for the regular occurrence of this dialectic as well as its result, is, according to Winnicott, a specific developmental stage. Bion, by contrast, relates to the interaction between the *emergent* and the *continuous* as an internal dynamic which, in different modes and variations, occurs in the human subject from the moment of birth and through the rest of one's life. Hence, it cannot be seen as a developmental stage and cannot reach a point of fulfillment.

One can say that while Winnicott conceives of the self as a *developing self*, Bion, in the footsteps of Melanie Klein, sees the self as a *becoming self*, or perhaps as an *ever becoming self*: a self whose incessant becoming actually constitutes its very essence.

Notes

1 Freud used this term to describe a neurophysiological synapse. Bion borrowed it to designate a structure that has both the functions of contact and of barrier. It is formed through the articulation of alpha elements that cohere as they proliferate. It is in a continuous process of formation and marks both the point of contact and separation between conscious and unconscious elements. They may cohere or agglomerate; be ordered sequentially as a narrative, as it happens in a dream; or, be ordered logically or geometrically. The contact barrier has the function of a semi-permeable membrane. It impedes phantasies from being overwhelmed by realistic facts and also protects contact with reality from being disturbed by emotions coming from inside. It acts as an articulating caesura that makes thinking and communication possible (Skelton, 2006).

2 Britton, in his paper "Keeping Things in Mind" (1992), also refers to these two elements.

References

Balint, M. (1968). *The Basic Fault*. London: Tavistock Publications.

Bion, W.R. (1962a). The Psycho-Analytic Study of Thinking. *International Journal of Psycho-Analysis*, 43, pp. 306–310.

Bion, W.R. (1962b). *Learning from Experience*. London: Heinemann. [Reprinted London: Karnac Books, 1984.]

Bion, W.R. (1967). Catastrophic Change. Unpublished paper.

Bion, W.R. (1970). Container and Contained. In *Attention and Interpretation*. London: Tavistock Publications [reprinted London: Karnac Books, 1984], pp. 72–82.

Britton, R. (1992). Keeping Things in Mind. *New Library of Psychoanalysis*, 14, pp. 102–113.

Klein, M. (1935). A Contribution to the Psychogenesis of Manic-Depressive States. In *The Writings of Melanie Klein, Volume 1*. London: Hogarth Press, pp. 262–289.

Klein, M. (1940). Mourning and its Relation to Manic-Depressive States. In *The Writings of Melanie Klein, Volume 1*. London: Hogarth Press, pp. 344–389.

Kulka, R. (1995), Revolutionary Continuity in Psychoanalysis. In *Winnicott: Playing and Reality* (Preface to the Hebrew version). Tel-Aviv: Am-Oved, pp. 229–242.

Ogden, T. (1986). *The Matrix of the Mind*. Northvale, NJ; London: Jason Aronson, Inc.

Skelton, R. (Ed.). (2006). *The Edinburgh International Encyclopaedia of Psychoanalysis*. Edinburgh: Edinburgh University Press.

Symington, J. and Symington, N. (1996). *The Clinical Thinking of Wilfred Bion*. London and New York: Routledge.

Winnicott, D.W. (1945) [1992]. Primitive Emotional Development. In *Through Pediatrics to Psychoanalysis*. New York: Basic Books, pp. 145–156.

Winnicott, D.W. (1951). Transitional Objects and Transitional Phenomena. In *Through Paediatrics to Psycho-Analysis: Collected Papers*. London: Tavistock Publications, 1958, pp. 140–152.

Winnicott, D.W. (1954–1955). The Depressive Position in Normal Development. In *Through Paediatrics to Psycho-Analysis: Collected Papers*. London: Tavistock Publications, pp. 262–277.

Winnicott, D.W. (1958). The Capacity To Be Alone. In *The Maturational Processes and the Facilitating Environment*. New York: International Universities Press, 1965, pp. 29–36.

Winnicott, D.W. (1960). Ego Distortion in Terms of True and False Self. In *The Maturational Processes and the Facilitating Environment*. New York: International Universities Press, 1965, pp. 140–152.

Winnicott, D.W. (1963). Communicating and Not Communicating Leading to a Study of Certain Opposites. In *The Maturational Processes and the Facilitating Environment*. New York: International Universities Press, 1965, pp. 179–192.

Winnicott, D.W. (1967). The Location of the Cultural Experience. In *Playing and Reality*. New York: Basic Books, 1971, pp. 95–103.

Winnicott, D.W. (1969). The Use of an Object. *International Journal of Psycho-Analysis*, 50, pp. 711–716.

Winnicott, D.W. (1971a). *Playing and Reality*. New York: Basic Books.

Winnicott, D.W. (1971b). The Use of the Object and Relating Through Cross-Identification. In *Playing and Reality*. New York: Basic Books, pp. 86–94.

2

THE EMERGENT, THE CONTINUOUS AND THE LYRICAL

The emergent self, the continuous self and their particular meanings within the dynamics of the psychic structure

What are the continuous self and the emergent self? The continuous principle of the self, which is in a perpetual dialogue with the rules of the common reality, is in charge of what we experience as dependent on external laws. This is the psychic part that is preoccupied by the common and the similar, not by the singular and the exceptional. It is the representation of finitude in the human psyche: identifying the similar and the common marks both the limit of omnipotence and the limit of subjectivity. The emergent principle of the self, on the other hand, is in charge of everything the psyche experiences as mutable, singular and distinct. By its very nature, the emergent represents a recurrent act of creation, and therefore the possibility to re-create again and again. In this sense this principle, which is in charge of the constant change, represents the psychic infiniteness.

D.B. Stern writes (2010):

> One way to define states of self is as narratives: Each state is an ever changing story [. . .] because self-states are not simply experiences or memories, but aspects of identity, each state is an aspect of self defined by the stories that can be told from within it. Our freedom to tell many self-stories at once – in other words, our freedom to inhabit multiple states of being simultaneously – is what gives to the stories that express the ways we know ourselves and others the plasticity to change with circumstances. The many states that compose the "me" not only participate in shaping the circumstances of my life, but are, in the process, themselves reshaped. This continuous interchange and renewal is the hallmark of the self-states that make up "me."
>
> *(Stern, 2010, p. 122)*

Stern's idea that human experience is "completely reformulated in every moment" and that "we are constantly making our experience anew" (Stern, 2013) is largely supported by findings from the neuroscience perspective that focus on explicit memory, for instance, as a dialectical and highly dynamic phenomenon in which we are shaping and reshaping our memories each time we allegedly "remember" them.

But the emergent principle is not in charge of merely our memories, but of our entire perception. The incessant experience of becoming, which is attributed to this emergent principle, is thus responsible also for the experience of anxiety and insecurity and for the sense of psychic "hole", constituting absence through its constant attack upon any sort of continuity. The mind dominated by the emergent principle may be described as very creative, but is often on the verge of becoming insane.

These two modes of experience: the emergent and the continuous, do not exist only one beside the other, but also one against the other. Indeed, the mind cannot endure the emergent in itself without the envelope that the continuous provides to it.

Not only the general personality, but each and every psychic event – whether located in the conscious or in the unconscious, whether encoded as a dream or as a memory – includes these two modalities. Every psychic phenomenon has its emergent aspect, which marks it as a new, singular and specific occurrence that can be neither foretold nor explained – and a continuous aspect, which simultaneously disposes it as part of continuity and in terms of causality and memory. The more enhancing and inspiring the interaction between the emergent self and the continuous self, the greater the degree of integration between them. What I refer to is not a binary between "yes integration" and "no integration", but a continuum stretching between states with a low level of integration and states with an optimal level of integration. It is the integration between the emergent and the continuous that constitutes what I call "the lyrical dimension of the psychic space", and the quality of this integration is what determines the quality of this dimension as well.

Why lyrical? Like in poetry, this lyrical dimension captures every experience from its most private, ineffable and inexplicable side, as well as its general, communicable one. One can say, for instance, that the inaugurating movement of the Winnicottian "potential space" – the movement between me and not-me (or the dialectic between the subjective and objective perceptions of any object) – can in fact be considered as a specific actualization of the interaction between the emergent and the continuous self; between what is experienced as the most unique, singular and ever-changing aspects of the self – and the inner representation of everything the self experiences as stable, predictable and imposed from outside. It is the quality of the interaction between, and integration of, emergent and continuous elements that influences every interaction between the self and the object.

This certainly evokes Noam Chomsky's (1957, 1968) notion of "deep structure". The crux of Chomsky's argument is that a person cannot possibly deduce and then apply the grammatical structure of language in the absence of a pre-existent system by means of which one can sort out and organize the wealth of sounds that one is exposed to. This system is what Chomsky calls "the deep structure of language". The individual person is not required to generate a grammar, nor indeed can he or she do so. Rather, the baby is born with a code that is part of his or her perceptual, cognitive and motor mechanisms. This code determines that the baby will organize perceptual input and make it linguistically meaningful in a very specific way.

Following Chomsky, I suggest that the human psyche also contains "a lyrical deep structure" or "a lyrical pre-conception", having an inborn predisposition to perceive the world in terms of the emergent and the continuous, and to achieve integration between them. The humans' psychic driving force, to a great extent, is the a priori inclination to achieve such integration. The "lyrical deep structure" is, in fact, that very mould of emergent/continuous interaction into which, at a later stage, the data of reality and experience are poured. The quality of the emergent/continuous interaction and integration is not only the result of the concrete interaction between the emergent and the continuous in the mother–child relations, for instance – but also the factor which determines the degree of integration and internalization of this concrete interaction. Eventually, the reciprocal relations between the given reality and the innate deep structure determine the quality of the lyrical dimension. Every object activates both the emergent dimension of the self – through which it is perceived in a new, unrecognized manner – as well as the continuous dimension that supplies it with an experience of continuity in terms of its "realistic" features. The ceaseless dialogue between the emergent and the continuous elements, between the common external dimension of every occurrence and the singular, ever-changing one – is what actually creates the sense of density and solidity of the mental space.

Ronald Britton, in his paper "Naming and Containing" (Britton, 1998a), offered an interesting variant of the notion of the container/contained relationship, describing the entire analytic situation as an attempt to provide "a well-defined world in which it is possible to find meaning" (p. 21). Without a sense of being sheltered – with "shelter" referring to the feeling that one is inside something safe – the individual experiences him or herself in free fall. If, then, one also loses the second of these features – namely meaning – this causes a sense of fragmentation and lack of inner coherence. This type of interaction, to which Britton refers to as the wish for "a well-defined world in which meaning can be found", is a very exact representation of the relationship between the emergent and the continuous principles of the self. While the continuous self is in charge of the stability and order that are determined by the rules of common reality, the emergent self looks after subjective, dynamic and free meaning with which it infuses the objective world.

Bion identified three possible types of such interaction between container and contained: commensal, symbiotic and parasitic. We may suppose that wherever the interaction between the emergent and the continuous principles of the self is parasitic in nature or takes the form of a "malignant containment" (Britton, 1998a,

p. 28), one of two things happens: the continuous self smothers the emergent self, leaving the latter no space for movement or development, or alternatively the emergent self stretches the continuous self beyond its breaking point and crashes through its boundaries. Bion (1970) argued that the sense of catastrophe that attends such an interaction between the emergent and the continuous is associated with the fact that the psychic space is unable to supply an experience of constancy beyond change; an experience that is actually the primary condition for change. When the continuous principle prevails, the psychic space becomes lacking in depth and resonance, while when the emergent principle takes over, the psychic space turns into a terrifying nightmare. If we use these two possibilities, with some caution, in order to formulate the development of certain types of psychopathology, we may say that the first one throws light on the development of the schizoid structure while the second elucidates the development of borderline and psychotic conditions. If, by contrast, the interaction is compatible – integration may occur, inaugurating the lyrical dimension of the psychic space.

In fact, not only the lyrical dimension of the psyche – but also the lyrical dimension of the analytic space can be reframed as representing various types of interaction between the emergent and the continuous principles. While the analytic setting may be seen as representing the continuous principle – that is, expressing the stable and static elements that are determined by external rules – the inner scene can be interpreted as representing the emergent principle that stages the analytic relations in a way that reflects the patient's inner world. In a very similar way, transference may be seen as the simultaneous combination of the continuous objective perception of the analyst as a stable external figure, while at the same time creating him or her in terms of the emergent self, i.e. featuring him or her into a different role every session anew. Analytic work should have the same elastic traits as the psyche itself in order to maintain itself as a creative space: not only to keep the boundaries, but also to stay open to the new meanings that those boundaries may adsorb; not to treat them as a self-evident knowledge, a static representation of the "establishment", but rather to enable the everlasting inner "messianic" movement to emerge through and between them.

In his essay "Revelation and Concealment in Language", Bialik, the Hebrew poet, writes:

> It has come to the point where the human language has become two languages [. . .]: one, an internal language, that of solitude and the soul, in which what is essential is "how?" as in music – the domain of poetry; the other, the external language, that of abstraction and generalization, in which the essential is "what?" as in mathematics – the domain of logic. Who knows whether it is not for the best that man should inherit the husk of a word without its core – for thus he can fill the husk, or supply it constantly from his own substance, and pour his own inner light into it. [. . .] In the final analysis, an empty vessel can hold matter, while a full vessel cannot; if the empty word enslaves, how much more is this true of the full word?
>
> (Bialik, 2000, pp. 14–15)

And further on:

> From all that has been said, it would appear that there is a vast difference
> between the language of the masters of prose and that of the masters of poetry.
> The former, the masters of exposition, find their sanction in the principles of
> analogy, and in the elements common to images and words, in that which
> is established and constant in language, in the expected version of things –
> consequently, they walk confidently through language. To what may they
> be compared? To one who crosses a river walking on hard ice frozen into a
> solid block. Such a man may and can divert his attention completely from the
> covered depths flowing underneath his feet. But their opposites, the masters
> of allegory, of interpretation and mystery, spend all their days in pursuit
> of the unifying principle in things, of the solitary something, of the point
> that makes one body of all the images, of the fleeting moment that is never
> repeated. They pursue their solitary inwardness and the personal quality of
> things. Therefore, the latter, the masters of poetry, are forced to flee all that
> is fixed and inert in language, all that is opposed to their goal of the vital
> and mobile in language. On the contrary, using their unique keys, they
> are obliged themselves to introduce into language at every opportunity –
> never-ending motion, new combinations and associations. The words writhe
> in their hands; they are extinguished and lit again, flash on and off like the
> engravings of the signet in the stones of the High Priest's breastplate, grow
> empty and become full, put off a soul and put on a soul.
>
> *(Bialik, 2000, pp. 24–25)*

And eventually:

> [O]ne mark, a change in the point of one iota, and the old word shines with
> a new light. The profane turns sacred, the sacred profane. Long established
> words are constantly being pulled out of their settings, as it were, and
> exchanging places with one another. Meanwhile, between concealments the
> void looms. And that is the secret of the great influence of the language of
> poetry. And to what may those writers be compared? To one who crosses
> a river when it is breaking up, by stepping across floating, moving blocks of
> ice. He dare not set his foot on any one block for longer than a moment,
> longer than it takes him to leap from one block to the next. And so on.
> Between the breaches the void looms, the foot slips, danger is close . . .
>
> *(Bialik, 2000, pp. 25–26)*

What is this abyss that Bialik refers to? It is the abyss of "the essence of things"
(p. 15): the very essence that language does not lead us into, but rather bars us from.
"On the other side of the barrier of language, behind its curtain, stripped of its husk
of speech, the spirit of man wanders ceaselessly", he writes (pp. 15–16), suggesting
that the essence of this spirit – the spirit in itself – cannot be captured in words.

"Knowledge and speech rule only over that which is on this side, within the four cubits of space and time", Bialik goes on (pp. 18–19), meaning that the laws of causality, time and space, the laws we impose on language and perception and by means of which we create the illusion of a "common reality", actually function as a cover for the deep essence of things, which neither is commonly shared nor obeys extraneous laws.

Bialik, however, does not refer to language in its concrete sense, but rather to its metaphorical sense as an allegory of the human psyche and its modes of existence and experience. The two languages that he mentions: the language of poetry and the language of prose, do not only mark the difference between the language of the story and that of the poem, but also the difference between the emergent mode of perception, in which the self experiences the world, both inside and outside, differently each moment, and the continuous mode of perception, which makes sense of the world by means of fixed and conventional rules.

Bialik identifies the "masters of exposition" – namely those who use prose, or who represent the *continuous self*, both in the external world and in the psychic realm – as those who "find their sanction in the principles of analogy, and in the elements common to images and words" (p. 24). If we transpose Bialik's words from language to the psychic field, and from the external world to the territory of the internal world, we can read them as stressing the "shared" nature of the continuous self, which is responsible for the exposed (what Bialik calls the "revealed") literal meaning. This literal meaning concerns things as they simply are and relies upon "the principles of analogy", which allows us to identify similarity, to generalize and to map both the internal and external world with reference to fixed and predictable rules.

Bialik contrasts this with "the masters of allegory, of interpretation and mystery", who "spend all their days in pursuit of the unifying principle in things", of the "solitary something", of the fleeting moment that can never be repeated. The emergent self, like those masters of poetry, flees all that is fixed and inert, all that is opposed to the vital and mobile. It is the representative of that which is eternally changing, in charge of the singular and astir, the "solitary inwardness and the personal quality of things", which by its very nature strays from the shared and conventional. Bialik does not argue that either one of these modes of expression, or the modes of perception they represent, should be preferred over the other. But he does assume that the poetic, which in this context is closer to the emergent self, offers more cracks to look into the deep essence of things. Approaching this essence, however, is not an experience that the psyche can undergo for any length of time. This is why the human subject invests such energies into covering the abyss. In terms of the psychic interaction between the emergent self and the continuous self, this can be formulated as follows: since life exclusively in the domain of the emergent self is insufferable, the psyche mobilizes the continuous self, which puts a limit to and a cover on the experience of pure change, of pure "new", thus making possible a "how" which is then filled by the "what" – rather than leaving just a "how" in itself, which would consign the self to unstructured, shapeless chaos.

The complex dialectic between the emergent and the continuous self can also be rendered in these terms: the "what" without the "how" remains vacant, barren and lifeless, while the "how" without the "what" remains chaotic, even psychotic. Recognizing the need for integration between these two principles beyond their dialectic, Bialik argues: "Who knows whether it is not for the best that man should inherit the husk of a word without its core – for thus he can fill the husk, or supply it constantly from his own substance, and pour his own inner light into it" (pp. 14–15). He further writes, taking us back to Bion's ideas concerning the container/contained relation: "In the final analysis, an empty vessel can hold matter, while a full vessel cannot; if the empty word enslaves, how much more is this true of the full word?" (pp. 14–15). Over-filled, the container will "stifle" the contained, while an empty container will allow the contained to fill it with its own singular meaning.

Bialik may have meant that a language whose words have petrified into their fixed meaning will not allow the speaker to insert his or her personal character and colour into its shared content. This language will allow him or her to speak *it*, but not to speak *in it*. And, in parallel: the psyche whose different components are charged exclusively with their common meaning is a psyche that lacks the ability to shift and to change. By contrast, a language whose words are charged exclusively with their singular meaning is a language that one can speak in – but not speak with. Such a language, even if it expresses a greater proximity to the "things in themselves" – to the abyss that is gaping below – cannot serve as a bridge over that abyss. And again, in parallel, the psyche which is dominated by the emergent self is not a psyche that can communicate either with the world of objects or with itself in terms of the worlds of objects. The most extreme version of this psychic type, the psychotic personality, is locked in its private world in an utter and tormented loneliness, in thrall to the experience of incessant change without being able to set a foot on an ice floe that won't shift or break.

Returning to Ronald Britton's formulation of the therapeutic situation as hinging on the wish for "a well-defined world in which it is possible to find meaning" (1998a, p. 21), we can say that if prose – the language of the continuous self – supplies the shelter of limits, poetry – the language of the emergent self – is what fills these limits with meaning. It is the poetic phrases in human expression that allow the self both the greatest freedom and the closest proximity to the language of childhood.

The prosaic passages, by contrast, are where the self sets limits so as to protect itself from falling apart. Though the poetic fills the prosaic with meaning, it is the prosaic that makes it possible for the poetic to exist freely and creatively without fear. The integration between the emergent and the continuous, between the poetic and the prosaic, forms the lyrical dimension, namely the dimension that configures the psyche itself as a lyrical space. Thus, the lyrical includes both the poetic and the prosaic. It is the integration between them that turns the psyche into a three-dimensional space that simultaneously contains both the limits and the movement between them; the abstract and the concrete; the wish and the ability to fulfill it.

James Grotstein, in his book *Who Is the Dreamer Who Dreams the Dream?*, divides dreaming into two functions – "the dreamer who dreams the dream", and "the dreamer who understands the dream":

> Bion, in his concept of the container and the contained, posited that the infant who is contained and the mother who contains him constitute a thinking couple. I believe that Bion's concept can be extended to include a dreaming couple.
>
> *(Grotstein, 2000, p. 6)*

There is a certain link between these two functions of dreaming and the emergent and continuous principles of the self. Grotstein refers to the process of dreaming alone, but since according to him the function of dreaming represents (in line with Bion's views) a very high degree of mental integration, his ideas can also be taken in a wider psychic context. In his above-quoted words he seeks to extend Bion's conception of the mother–child dyad as a "thinking couple" into one of a "dreaming couple". I would like to suggest that this concept could be extended once more to include a "lyrical couple". Much like the mother's breast or face can be thought of as "a dream-screen container" (Grotstein, 2000, p. 6) that welcomes the emergence of the dream on its surface, it is possible to think of the continuous self – the representation of the maternal container within the lyrical dimension – as the part that welcomes the movement of the emergent self within its stable boundaries, thus enabling a lyrical integration. The mother's breast, or her face, is not a blank screen as Grotstein's formulation may suggest: it has its own a priori qualities and constraints. Similarly, we can say that the continuous self, which serves as a container for the emergent self, is not merely a container that has a priori limitations (depending on its rigidity or fragility), but also represents by its very nature the existence of constraint and boundary as such.

According to Grotstein, the function of "rewriting the dream", which in fact is responsible for the appearance of the dream as such, belongs to what he calls "the dreamer who understands the dream". This, among other things, is responsible for self-reflection:

> As I understand the legend of Genesis, it was important for the God-child, having just been born, to imagine that He created all that His eyes opened to before He could allow for the separate creation of His perceptions.
>
> *(Grotstein, 2000, pp. 7–8)*

This certainly fits with Winnicott's approach concerning the infant's need at the outset of life for a subjective creation of objects, before being able to perceive their objective existence. Can it be argued, equally, that the emergent self somehow precedes the continuous self? The emergent and the continuous both exist in the human psyche as innate predispositions. From the moment of his or her birth, the baby engages in the internalization, on the basis of these predispositions, of emergent and continuous data, as well as those concerning the ongoing interaction between them. What we have here is a parallel and complementary process in the course of which the continuous principle in the human psyche constitutes the emergent while the emergent constitutes the continuous at the very same time: a container/contained relationship in which the continuous serves as a container to the emergent, while the emergent simultaneously fills the continuous with meaning. Every container/contained relationship encapsulates elements of mutual constitution.

Similarly, it is not just the mother who "creates" the child in her womb, but the child's being in her womb also "creates" or constitutes her as a mother. And much like the child grows more creative in proportion to the degree of security and value provided by the caring adult, so does the emergent principle gain freedom of action and a wider range of motion as the continuous principle offers it a sense of protection within its stable boundaries. It is upon the continuous principle, within this complex dialectic, to confirm the emergent principle's singular value, as well as its boundaries and constraints. Only within safe boundaries will the emergent aspect be able to create the individual experience without becoming dominant and destructive. What protects the self from psychosis – which can be understood as the emergent self prevailing over the continuous self – is a continuous self that constitutes boundaries, but also allows for freedom of expression within them. What, by contrast, safeguards the self from neurosis, or from cognitive rigidity and affective barrenness – is an emergent self that fills these boundaries with meaning and content, and whose very movement within the continuous boundaries generates psychic volume, thus constituting psychic space.

This is easily illustrated by looking at the dream as a moment of lyrical integration: what keeps the dream from turning into a psychotic delirium is the continuous principle, which is responsible for the ability to wake up into a continuous and ongoing experience of selfhood. What, on the other hand, enables the creative movement within the dream and hence renders the dream meaningful is the emergent principle, which pours its singular and private meaning into this selfhood. Thus, the dream space is the result of the interaction and integration between these two principles of the self; it is what stretches between the dream as a private experience in which the self contains the world in its own subjectivity, and the point at which the dream also serves as an introspective tool by means of which the individual observes the world from a reflective point of view.

Somewhat reminiscent of Winnicott's (1971) two phases of object use, it can be said that if the achievement that marks the beginning of psychic development is the freedom to evolve an emergent self – the achievement that marks later stages of development is the self's (*continuous*) ability to observe itself in terms of common reality. I do not mean to argue that the continuous principle is the "product" of a later development. The emergent principle and the continuous principle are both internalized and re-internalized through an ongoing dynamic process starting at the very beginning of life. Yet at the start of life (and this bears some similarity to the beginning of the therapeutic process too) the emergent dominates over the continuous, while at later stages of development the continuous grows more dominant until it finally forms itself as a container whose stability makes the creative and free existence of the emergent principle possible.

The mother–infant dyad and the therapist–patient dyad actually represent the same dialectic relation between the emergent and the continuous elements: in the absence of infantile omnipotence, human existence will remain empty and barren. Omnipotence, at the same time though, must stay contained within the awareness of the finality and partiality of physical and psychological existence. It is the free child within the psyche who builds the inner responsible adult, much like the subjective creation of the world of objects at the onset of life serves as the basis for the constitution of an objective experience of both self and external world.

When Grotstein moves on to the second function of the dream work, the one he calls *the dreamer who understands the dream*, he writes:

> I reasoned that there must be something like an unseen audience in the dream who observes the play, experiences its truths and its messages, and renders an approval that vouchsafes the continuation of sleep.
>
> *(Grotstein, 2000, p. 9)*

This certainly accords with the assumption of a stable and fixed principle (which I have been calling the continuous self) that takes responsibility for reality testing and the experience of sequence and continuity.

Grotstein goes on:

> The dream is a passion play [. . .] in the rhythmic concordance between the dream actor and the dream audience, [. . .] the effect of the audience's certification is to establish a boundary to curtail omnipotent performance, passionate penetrations and, conversely, to authenticate those aspects of the emerging "I" which are worthy of "truth" and realness.
>
> *(Grotstein, 2000, p. 11)*

And he concludes:

> *The Dreamer Who Understands the Dream* is the audience that verifies the passion of the dreamer. In addition to being the requisitioner of the dream, it is also the barrier that contains the dream. It functions as a porous mirror to reflect the passions of the dreamer but also to be influenced by them, much like a mother's relationship to a child.
>
> *(Grotstein, 2000, p. 11)*

Grotstein is not talking about static relations. On the contrary, he argues that an infinite number of encoded messages are likely to move back and forth between *the dreamer who dreams the dream* and *the dreamer who understands the dream*, and this reciprocal, dynamic process eventually comes to shape what he calls *an acceptable dream narrative*. I argue, similarly, that the "acceptable" experience of selfhood is the product of an incessant reciprocal motion and an endless interaction between the emergent and the continuous within the self. The continuous, within this oscillation, serves as a boundary and container to the emergent while the emergent charges the continuous with content and meaning.

Both the *dreamer who dreams the dream* and *the dreamer who understands the dream* take part in the sense of I-ness, argues Grotstein. Together they compose the subjective sense of self which is capable of experiencing the realness and truth within the dream. Hence, under normal circumstances, we can think of the *dreamer who dreams the dream* and *the dreamer who understands the dream* as operating conjointly, allowing the dreamer to have a sense of continuous identity. If the dreamer's experience of I-ness were to rely on one part of the *dreaming couple*, or on one part of the *lyrical couple*, in parallel, it would be reduced to a two-dimensional experience. As such, it would constitute a certain experience of *self*, yet never become an experience of *selfhood*: a three-dimensional experience that contains not only the planar movement between omnipotence and impotence and between infinitude and finitude, but also (or mainly) the ability to experience these simultaneously, not as extremes of a continuum but as different dimensions of the same existential experience.

What this implies is that if the planar radius of the self indeed stretches between these poles of experience, then *selfhood* is the additional dimension that emerges when we "fold" this two-dimensionality by integrating these poles, thus creating depth, or in fact, an interior. The lyrical dimension of the psychic space creates the experience of selfhood that is beyond the self, much like the mutual collaboration between *the dreamer who dreams the dream* and *the dreamer who understands the dream* eventually creates the experience of "a dreamer" beyond the dream. Only within the context of selfhood do the diverse aspects of experience transform from being opposites whose attributes clash (i.e. impede integration) into ones whose attributes are mutually complementary and can therefore be linked.

In his paper "Objectivity, Subjectivity, and Triangular Space" (1998b), Ronald Britton follows Bion in formulating the destructive transition from a person's momentary experience of "not being understood" into a generalized experience of "being incomprehensible". I would like to use this formulation, though slightly reversed, to explain what I mean by "the experience of selfhood that is beyond the self". The experience of selfhood is the integration of all the momentary experiences of the self. The sense that "one is incomprehensible" is not tantamount to the sum of moments during which one has felt oneself "not understood". Rather, it is a generalization that exceeds the sum of these moments and becomes a kind of *formative experience*: an experiential mould into which one will pour from now on every new experience and by means of which he or she will render such experiences meaningful. Selfhood is never an accumulation of momentary thoughts or perceptions ("X loves me" or "Y does not understand me") but an integration of these thoughts or perceptions ("I am worthy of love" or "I am not understandable"). It is the ability to integrate isolated experiences and make them meaningful through this integration that forms the basis of the experience of selfhood. This ability is the result of the integration of the emergent and the continuous principles of the self.

Why is it that the experience of selfhood ensues from the integration of these principles?

The ability to draw a link between discrete perceptions is a characteristic of the continuous principle, which is responsible for identifying the shared and the similar. The ability to infuse singular meaning into each such separate experience is a feature of the emergent principle. However, the ability to cluster together discrete experiences, with their unique, singular meanings as well as what they share, and to bind them into one unified experience that transcends them, is exactly what characterizes the lyrical dimension. The conjunction between these two principles – one supplying the singular data and the other supplying the common link – is what enables the integration of the mass of discrete perceptions into an experience of continuous selfhood.

When we lean our body against a hard surface, for example a wall, we do not solely feel the wall. We feel our back too. In the same way, we feel our hand when it touches something other than itself, or when it is made to feel pain by an outside source. What this amounts to is that in order to have an experience of ourselves, we need to be in touch with something we experience as external to ourselves. Thus, we experience our emergent self only when it is in touch with the continuous. The continuous is not only the context within which the emergent arises but also what makes the existence of the emergent possible due to its contact with it.

In the note "What Objective Unity of Self-Consciousness Is" (Kant, 1934, p. 98), Immanuel Kant talks about the fact that the mental act of association ("association of representation") is possible only because the transcendental I, that is, the general, stable I that joins between images and identifies objects, provides the matrix that enables personal associations that are subjectively valid, as well as accidental associations. Thus, the self's experience of coherence and continuity, according to Kant too, depends on the interaction of consciousness – which is in charge of the experience of "being identical to oneself" – with the principle that is in charge of constant change, of singularity and specificity. The experience of identity or selfhood eventually includes these two features: the outer shell that is fixed beyond all change, responsible for identity in the sense of *being identical* and the endless movement that is in charge of the *identity* in the sense of distinctness and singularity.

What, then, enables us to reflect upon ourselves?

The emergent, naturally, cannot observe itself. The ability to observe assumes constancy, while the emergent undergoes incessant change. It is, hence, the continuous that affords us the vantage point that enables reflection. From the continuous vantage point we can observe the emergent and grasp it, while we cannot look at the continuous from the vantage point of the emergent. Constituting the fixed point within our perceptions, the continuous is the benchmark by means of which we can assess size, time and distance. And yet it is not the continuous principle but the lyrical dimension that forms the reflecting part: if the emergent is the view that changes with every blink of our eye and the continuous is the vantage point, then the lyrical dimension is the gaze that contains both the dramatic change of the entire view each and every moment and the stable position from which we look at these shifts. It is the emergent principle that generates the sense of the specificity and singularity of every data of sensual input, while the continuous principle makes for the sense of generality and commonness of these data, and hence creates the experience of regularity and order: this differs from that, this happened before that, this was the cause of that.

The experience of meaningfulness, however, is created by the lyrical dimension, which unites the general order with the singular one. While we are looking down at the valley below, the emergent is the landscape that constantly changes as our gaze passes over it. The continuous, by contrast, is the knowledge that both the square of golden sunlight on the ground and the dark triangle of treetops to its left are parts of the very same valley. But the lyrical is the whole experience of the valley: it contains both the gaze which each moment lights upon a different fragment of the view, perceiving it as a world unto itself, and the knowledge that all this is part of something that actually exists outside our gaze and perception. The continuous is the internal reflection or the internal by-product of the experience that there is something outside the psyche; a reality whose existence does not rely on ours and extends beyond us. This assumption is so fundamental to the human experience, since it contains the assumption of our existence as objects and not merely as subjects. The continuous is the inner reflection of this assumption, or this experience, because it essentially relates to this exact aspect of sensory impressions: it constitutes the experience that there are "things as they are in themselves", while the experience of which the emergent is in charge is that there are only "things as they are to ourselves".

References

Bialik, H.N. (2000). *Revealment and Concealment, Five Essays*, trans. Zali Gurevitch. Jerusalem: Ibis Editions, German Colony.

Bion, W.R. (1970). Container and Contained. In *Attention and Interpretation*. London: Tavistock Publications [reprinted London: Karnac Books, 1984], pp. 72–82.

Britton, R. (1998a). Naming and Containing. In *Belief and Imagination*. London: Routledge, in association with the Institute of Psychoanalysis, pp. 19–28.

Britton, R. (1998b). Subjectivity, Objectivity and Triangular Space. In *Belief and Imagination*. London: Routledge, in association with the Institute of Psychoanalysis, pp. 41–58.

Chomsky, N. (1957). *Syntactic Structures*. The Hague: Mouton.

Chomsky, N. (1968). *Language and Mind*. New York: Harcourt, Brace and World.

Grotstein, J.S. (2000). *Who Is the Dreamer Who Dreams the Dream?* New Jersey and London: The Analytic Press.

Kant, I. (1934). *Critique of Pure Reason*, trans. J.M.D.Meiklejohn. London: Everyman's Library.

Stern, D.B. (2010). *Partners in Thoughts: Working with Unformulated Experience, Dissociation and Enactment*. New York: Routledge.

Stern, D.B. (2013). Relational Freedom and Therapeutic Action. *Journal of American Psychoanalysis*, 61, pp. 227–255.

Winnicott, D.W. (1971). *Playing and Reality*. New York: Basic Books.

3

THE PHILOSOPHICAL AND HUMAN MEANING OF THE LYRICAL DIMENSION

The poet T.S. Eliot (1944) once claimed that humankind cannot bear very much reality. What did he have in mind? Could he have intended that a too dominant continuous principle – which leads to an existence with too little "emergence" – might leave the psyche barren and sterile? Did he mean that an overly realistic perception – that is, relating to things too much in terms of their fixed aspect, while enabling too little of their creation in singular terms – is not within the scope of human possibility? For the profound role of the lyrical dimension is exactly this: it is the dimension that shields us from too much reality. It has this quality of allowing the psyche to bear reality because it supplies that psyche with the ability to experience reality as not merely a given imposed from without, but also as something that comes from within.

This chapter is dedicated therefore to a discussion of the philosophical and human significance of the lyrical dimension and the manner in which it renders human existence meaningful. For this purpose, two main categories will be discussed, to whose integration the lyrical dimension is especially relevant. These are the categories of the *possible* and the *actual*.

Amihud Gilead, in his book *Saving Possibilities* (1999), proposes a new way of thinking about the ancient question of body and mind. While the mental and the physical are not identical, they are most intimately connected. This complex psychophysical unity conceives of a distinction between the mentally "possible" and the physically "actual". While preserving the categorical distinction between body and mind, this division also simultaneously ensures and confirms the necessary connection between them. Gilead suggests conceiving of the mental as belonging to the category of the possible, and the physical as ranging under the category of the actual (the realized). Since the actual is also possible, but not everything that is possible is also actual – the possible is a broader category than the actual and includes and encompasses it. Gilead, in this context, attributes singularity to the psyche only, not to the body, and his writings deal extensively with the uniqueness of psychological possibilities (Gilead, 1999, 2003).

Unlike Gilead, I would like to suggest that there is, within the psychic realm, a similar division between the actual self, which is the actualized part of mental life (whether conscious or unconscious) and the possible self – the singular part that is present in the form of an unrealized psychic possibility. It should be stressed that the realm of the possible in the case of one person is never like that of another, nor does anyone ever fully realize their possibilities. The actual is only a partial expression of the possible. Still, the quality of mental life depends on the extent and quality of the actualization of the possible.

But how does the psyche "select" whatever it is in the possible that will become actual? I suggest that the dimension in charge of the process of selection, or of the transition from the possible to the actual, is the lyrical dimension. The type of integration that constitutes the lyrical dimension – the integration between knowing the boundaries and the freedom of creation within those boundaries – is the type of integration that the psyche uses when turning the possible into the actual or culling from the possible that which will be actualized.

In this process of selection, the two most crucial parameters are singularity and necessity: the first parameters to be chosen will be those that are the most singular within the specific psychic structure and distinguish it from any other. They are then unconsciously tested to check the extent of their necessity for maintaining this psychic structure. Identifying what is singular is fundamentally related to the emergent self. Pinpointing the necessary, by contrast, presupposes the existence of the continuous self. This is why I consider the integration of emergent and continuous – that is, the lyrical dimension – as the mechanism that allows for and structures the transition from the possible to the actual. Thus, the first to undergo actualization will be those parts that are the most "necessary" to the self's singularity, i.e. to its distinct identity, and these will be followed, in order of importance, by other, less necessary parts. The kind of necessity I am referring to is similar to the inner necessity of the creative act: the artist, on the one hand, enjoys the absolute freedom to create whatever comes to mind. On the other hand, however, he or she is bound to inner necessity, which while being reconcilable with creative freedom also furnishes the readers, listeners or spectators with the feeling that every detail in this work of art is in its exact and only place, and that if one of the details were either moved elsewhere or left out, the quality of the entire piece would suffer. Since the emergent/continuous integration is responsible for the identification of what is singular, as well as for the constraints on the actualization of this singularity, it is also in charge of the unconscious choice of the necessary conditions as well as of the sufficient conditions for the embodiment of the specific self. As said above, this selection is not made out of a general and shared stockpile (i.e. identical for all humans), but rather out of an a priori possible one, which is specific to each and every individual.

The implications of this process of selection and actualization of psychic components do not merely refer to the actualization of the possible. They also play a role in the self's ability to stay in touch with the possible components that have not become actualized, while not getting either flooded by or deprived of them. There is some similarity between this mechanism and the (previously discussed) "contact barrier" that allows the delicate trickling of the emergent into the continuous. If the seepage of the emergent into the continuous allows for dry details or facts to become charged with a singular meaning, the seepage of the possible into the actual allows for the text (the actual) to become enriched with a dimension of context. This second process is the continuation of the first and derives from it. Much like the emergent is contained by the continuous as a sense of depth – the possible (the dimension that folds "what could have been" into "what is") is encapsulated in the actual as a sense of colour.

What is the relationship between the actual/possible and the emergent/continuous?

The possible and the actual do not constitute alternative or parallel categories to the emergent and the continuous. The continuous is not identical to the actual, but rather the psychic mechanism that enables the self to recognize the actual through its organizing and structuring rules. It is the emergent, by contrast, that enables the self to be in touch with the possible: by representing the ever changing, that which is created differently each and every time, the emergent contains the world as an unending possibility.

The emergent/continuous relation is not identical to the internal/external relation as well; it actually consists of two lengthwise cross-sections that cut through both inner and outer reality: the emergent grasps both the internal and external in terms of their emergent qualities, while the continuous does so in terms of their continuous attributes. The process of internalization (the transformation of the external object to an internal one), for instance, is not a kind of "return" from the continuous to the emergent but rather a return from the actual to the possible: the internalized object does not divest itself of its continuous features, but of its actual ones. If it did the former – namely rid itself of its continuous features – it would have undergone a psychotic fragmentation. The change that the internalized object undergoes, therefore, does not occur on the level of integration between emergent and continuous, but on that of the relationship between the possible and the actual. The internalized object preserves its actual features in the form of memories, but they become extended in the process of internalization so that the possible comes to dominate in the process no less (and sometimes much more) than the actual.

This mechanism may explain how in many cases in which the actual functioning of the parental primary object was far from sound, it was nevertheless internalized as a good object. A child that has succeeded in developing (for partly constitutional reasons) "a good enough lyrical dimension", may have succeeded in the course of internalization to be in touch with the object's possible features and not just with its actual ones. In this way, the son of a depressive mother might have been able to register her possible care for him over and beyond the walls of her dysfunction; or, a child with a remote father could thus sense the possible tenderness that did not find an actual expression, but was present in the parental object as a possibility. What I am really arguing is that the process of internalization may protect the child from the actual destructiveness of the object, or, alternatively, it may expose the possible destructiveness behind an outer shell of actual sound functionality. This function of the lyrical dimension in the process of internalization is relevant both to diverse processes of mourning as well as to all types of significant relations.

Much like there is no parallel between emergent/continuous interaction and possible/actual interaction, there is, similarly, none between emergent/continuous relation and conscious/unconscious relation. Both the conscious and the unconscious have continuous as well as emergent features. The unconscious (in its Freudian definition) is a reservoir of repressed experiences. Each such experience, prior to being repressed, was absorbed in the conscious psyche, both in terms of its continuous aspect – that is, in terms of its conventional meaning – and in those of its emergent aspect, i.e. of its singular meaning. Each experience that is situated in the unconscious, therefore, includes these two dimensions as well as the dialectic between them. The emergent/continuous relation cuts, therefore, through all other categories of psychic existence.

It should already have become clear from the above that the lyrical dimension is not the artistic dimension of the human psyche – though artistic creation undoubtedly relies on its formation. It touches on a wide array of psychic functions that are related to the self's ability to regulate and adjust, as well as to its sense of truthfulness, its sense of depth and volume and its ability to connect between desire and object both in the external and in the internal world. The lyrical dimension is not necessarily the psychic capacity by means of which poetry is written. But it is certainly the capacity to extract poetry out of ordinary life by enabling each individual to constitute his or her unique variation of being.

In his article "The Other Room and Poetic Space" (1998), Ronald Britton develops the notion of the *other room* as the space of imagination and fiction. He suggests that the other room emerges as the subject imagines the parents' intercourse rather than observes their actual sexual relations. This is about the unwitnessed primal scene rather than the actual one: the one that we have imagined as happening in our absence; the one that exists only in our imagination and therefore becomes the space for fiction.

Unlike Winnicott, who defined the transitional phenomenon as the psychological space that arises from the relations between the infant and the mother, and hence is situated between "me" and "not-me", Britton argues that the creative space emanates from the internal triangular space. Similar to Melanie Klein (1924) and Otto Rank (1915) who argued that the origins of the theatrical stage are in the imaginary location of the parental sexual act, Britton claims that there is a "primal romantic couple", a "phantasised ideal, super-sexual parental couple", consisting of mythical figures, a kind of primal Adam and Eve, who are "the stars of the screen and the objects of endless media voyeurism". Having been expelled from Heaven, we are compelled, as non-participating observers, to imagine *their* Paradise. Paradise is our other room, forever unfulfilled with pain of longing (pp. 122–123).

What distinguishes between the poetic space and the lyrical dimension?

While the other room is a certain "location" or "space" within the psyche, the lyrical dimension is a "trait" that characterizes the entire potential space. Rather than being a feature that uniquely characterizes the other room, it is the dimension that constitutes both the possibility of the other room and *this room*, and thus enables the integration and dialectic between them. The poetic space – or the other room – is the space inside of which the whole range of creative activity flourishes. In this context Britton also differentiates between various personality types: those who don't visit their other room at all, whom he describes as "lacking in imagination"; as opposed to others, whose psychic barrier between this room and the other room has collapsed, resulting in a psychotic blurring of the distinction between fantasy and reality.

The lyrical dimension of the potential space, by contrast, is not characteristic merely of the activities that mobilize human creative powers. It is essential to psychic existence at all times – from when one engages in the most technical activities to when one reaches for the deepest roots of one's creativity. This is because in order to survive the simplest technical actions, one must maintain a sense of being more than the sum of these actions. One must preserve the possible that is enfolded within the actual (Gilead, 1999, 2003). In this sense, one may be in greater need of the lyrical dimension when folding the laundry than when writing a poem. Not because it is not possible to fold laundry without it, but rather because without it our experience will be reduced to nothing but the activity of this folding.

The lyrical dimension may be seen as a contextual dimension, since it supplies the possible context that endows the actual text with meaning. It is thanks to the lyrical dimension that the mechanical act of folding laundry is subsumed into the lyrical order of love. Without that, there would remain nothing but the Sisyphean motion between heaps of dirty laundry and piles of clean laundry; a meaningless motion, exhausting and frustrating, that turns the human subject into a slave of his or her banal existence. From this planar motion, the lyrical dimension releases another dimension: that of meaningfulness. Due to the ability to endow meaning, it becomes possible to grasp that the act of washing, like many others, addresses a most fundamental wish, namely that for a home. Once it is possible to grasp this, the Sisyphean aspect of the act loses its impact. Since the aim is not the concrete one of *clean laundry* but the lyrical one of a *sense of a home*, both folding away the clean laundry and washing the soiled clothes serve this purpose to the same extent.

Humankind indeed cannot bear too much reality, as said T.S. Eliot (1944). If we are not able to fill the simplest activities with their lyrical meaning, we will not be able to survive their banality. The profoundest significance of the lyrical dimension is therefore its most quotidian and simple one. The person whose lyrical dimension has sustained damage is doomed to experience him or herself as a heap of beads whose string has broken, like a scattering of words without syntax, a text without context that therefore fails to become etched into an experience of continuity and meaningfulness. Such a person will be locked in daily existence as in a psychic jail, holding on to the actions themselves while transposing symbolic meaning with concrete movement (a solution typical of situations where the continuous dominates the emergent). Alternatively, he or she will flee any type of constructive activity in favor of a wayward wandering in the labyrinthine world of his psyche (a solution that characterizes the situations where the emergent dominates the continuous). In either case, he or she will lack the experience of psychic volume, which renders a sense of fullness and presence.

The following words from Albert Camus's *The Myth of Sisyphus* are strikingly relevant:

> All Sisyphus' silent joy is contained therein. His fate belongs to him. His rock is his thing. Likewise, the absurd man, when he contemplates his torment, silences all the idols. In the universe suddenly restored to its silence, the myriad wondering little voices of the earth rise up. Unconscious, secret calls, invitations from all the faces, they are the necessary reverse and price of victory.
>
> *(Camus, 1955, p. 123)*

Sisyphus' joy is the result of his ability to turn "his rock" (i.e. his fate) into "his thing", his object of desire, his choice. In fact, the rock can be seen as tantamount to the data of reality as Sisyphus' continuous self perceives them. In this world, which consists of the sum of its "fixed" data, Sisyphus is locked in a useless and hopeless effort. He will never be able to vanquish gravity, which causes the rock to roll down each time Sisyphus manages to push it up to the top of the mountain. Never will he be able to diminish the huge effort needed to push the rock upwards once more, against its weight which pulls it down again and again. Gravity, the force in the face of which Sisyphus directs his tragic and absurd struggle, acts from without. As long as it is experienced as such, the force of the absurd continues to exhaust Sisyphus from within. The alternative Camus offers us is Sisyphus' power to reflect on the torture which he endures, and to transform, through this reflective capacity, what has been externally imposed into what was chosen and yearned for from within. Sisyphus does not distort reality, nor does he try to rebel against his fate by hurling the rock far away. Rather, he uses his capacity to rearrange the relations between the various elements in the scene.

The real director of this scene is the lyrical dimension of Sisyphus' psychic space. Its continuous aspect is what takes into account those elements of the scene that cannot be changed (the rock, the mountain, the force of gravity). Its emergent aspect is what allows Sisyphus to bestow his own meaning on each of these elements and their interrelations. As a result of the combined workings of these two, the countless fixed data of Sisyphus' existence can be placed on axes of value and meaning. "Each atom of that stone, each mineral flake of that night-filled mountain, in itself forms a world", writes Camus. "The struggle itself towards the heights is enough to fill a man's heart. One must imagine Sisyphus happy" (Camus, 1955, p. 123).

In a world whose "continuous" data are predetermined, whose laws and rules are not subject to change, human lyricism creates a space that enables movement by enriching even inevitable actions with a sense of freedom, significance and choice.

The integration of which the lyrical dimension is in charge constitutes not only the tool by means of which the psyche turns the possible into the actual, but also the one that extracts the possible from the actual. The lyrical extracts (extracts out of them, never imposes on them) the internal meaning enfolded in every external detail. The mother's lyrical dimension is what releases whatever is enfolded in her child as a possibility. What the mother of a disabled child loves about him or her is not just the actual child – the child that he or she is – but also the possible child – the child that he or she could have been. This implies something substantially different from the work of memory. In other words, this is not a case of a mother who holds in her memory what the child was for her before he became disabled. While memory is always of the actual – even if this is an actuality that was disrupted or obliterated – here we are dealing with a mother who by means of her love holds what has never been realized.

But the lyrical act of extracting the possible from the actual is relevant not only to parent-child or love relationships but also to the relationship between patient and analyst. The analyst's ability to identify the possible within the actual, both in oneself and in one's patients, is not a mere result of the analytic space, but something that is crucial for creating this space. This is very different from identifying unconscious contents. While the unconscious belongs to the actual, to the realized, though it comes without conscious knowing – here we are dealing with the ability to identify what resides in patients as a possibility without actual embodiment, and therefore can only be released from them through the analyst's use of his or her own lyrical dimension.

The lyrical dimension is what enables us to experience our movement in the actual world, not merely as progressing ahead, from birth to death, but also as directed inward. By adding the axis of meaning to the axis of existence, a singular experience that transcends factual, actual details arises. While factual details are always arranged on the time axis, the singular is situated on the axis of meaning. This is not a mode of storage but rather a mode of extraction: the lyrical dimension does not store details under various concepts or names as if it were filing a random collection of items into a storage cabinet. It rather places them on axes of meaning, in a similar way to stringing beads on a thread in order to create a chain. One may argue that the bead string is an artifice that comes to compensate for the truth concerning the beads' basic lack of coherence and meaning. My argument is that the string releases the true nature of the beads. It reveals the fact that it is in the nature of the beads – beyond their diverse and accidental shapes – to be strung. The lyrical mode of reflection divulges the object of our gaze, not only in its actual aspects, but also in its possible ones. For the lyrical person, it is enough to look at a fruit in order to experience the entire range of flavours that it includes – not just as a memory but as a possibility as well.

Amihud Gilead wrote in this context:

> Under love, we always long or yearn for our loved ones. Even in their actual presence, we still miss something of them, for we miss what is purely possible about them, or what is still possible but not actual about them.
>
> *(Gilead, 2003, pp. 439–440)*

At the end of his discussion of the various components of the process of dreaming, Grotstein directs his attention to the final one, which he calls "the dreamer who makes the dream understandable". The dream, he argues, uses its sender – "the dreamer who dreams the dream" – to convey the autochthonically imaginative creation known as the dream narrative to the "dreamer who understands the dream", who is an arcane representation of an internal containing object. Together they form the differentiation between sleep and wakefulness, needed not only to maintain sanity but also for the formation of a protective barrier between the perceptual functions of background and foreground (Grotstein, 2000, p. 30). If the dreamer's personality is full of confidence as a result of one's use of reverie, and if one can postpone his or her "rendezvous with the things-in-themselves", it is because he or she experiences themselves as containing an internal *dreaming couple* consisting of a competent mother/container and a spontaneous self. One partner in this couple is "the dreamer who dreams the dream" and the other is "the dreamer who understands the dream". By internalizing the dreaming couple, the child develops confidence in his ability to know both internal and external reality.

Grotstein believes that this process occurs close to the transition from "the omnipotent thinking couple" to "a real thinking couple". Eventually, a function develops that corresponds to the intrinsic analyst within us all. This is "the dreamer who makes the dream understandable". This, Grotstein argues, is Joseph the dreamer, Joseph who understands that things-in-themselves, while not omnipotent, are significant and offer necessary perspectives of truth. This is the observer who oversees the unfolding of the scenario. Together, he and his partner – "the dreamer who is willing to have his dream understood" – are in charge of mitigating the omnipotent powers and translating them into human language (Grotstein, 2000, p. 31).

The "dreamer who makes the dream understandable" is a function that is based upon the integration of "the dreamer who dreams the dream" and "the dreamer who understands the dream". By my understanding, this function is Grotstein's version of what I call the *lyrical dimension* of the psychic space. It is the dimension that enables us to recognize the finality of life, but at the same time understand that the road to psychic eternity passes through meaning. It is the dimension that makes it possible for us to maintain our optimism without losing our ability to grasp reality and its constraints: to enumerate the actual constellation of facts while also holding on to our faith and dreams.

References

Britton, R. (1998). The Other Room and Poetic Space. In *Belief and Imagination*. London: Routledge, in association with the Institute of Psychoanalysis, pp. 120–127.

Camus, A. (1955). *The Myth of Sisyphus and Other Essays*, trans. Justin O'Brie. New York: Alfred A. Knopf.

Eliot, T.S. (1944). *Four Quartets*. London: Faber and Faber.

Gilead, A. (1999). *Saving Possibilities: A Study in Philosophical Psychology*. Amsterdam: Rodopi.

Gilead, A. (2003). How Does Love Make the Ugly Beautiful? *Philosophy and Literature*, 27(2), pp. 436–443.

Klein, M. (1924). An Obsessional Neurosis in a Six-Year-Old Girl. In *The Writings of Melanie Klein, Volume 2*, R. Money-Kyrle, B. Joseph, E. O'Shaughnessy, H. Segal, Eds. London: The Hogarth Press, 1975, pp. 65–93.

Rank, O. (1915). Das Schauspiel im Hamlet. *Imago*, 4.

4

THE EMERGENT SELF AND
THE CONTINUOUS SELF IN THE
MIRROR OF DEVELOPMENT

Among the first questions that arise when thinking about the continuous and the emergent self is whether we are dealing with developmental stages or whether one of these aspects of the self has developmental priority over the other. It is tempting to assume that the emergent self precedes the continuous self. This would fit in well both with Winnicott's transition from a *subjective object* to *object relation*, as well as with Klein's developmental shift from the *schizoid-paranoid position* to the *depressive position*. While, however, certain parts of what I will argue below are indeed consonant with Winnicott's and Klein's developmental approaches, the principal assumption behind the concept of the lyrical dimension is that both the emergent and the continuous elements are present as pre-dispositions even before birth: they serve, as mentioned above, as deep-structures or as moulds into which real experiential data are poured.

From the very beginning of the infant's life, each time there is an interaction with the primary object, an interaction between the continuous and the emergent occurs and is internalized. This is not merely the apparently simple situation in which the mother (who is usually the primary object) functions as a continuous stable container within which the infant's emergent self takes shape.[1] Rather, it is an endless, dynamic process in which, each moment and again and again, a continuous with certain features, an emergent with certain features and a specific interaction between them are internalized. The mother, here, does not serve as a continuous only, nor is she internalized as such. The situation is far more complex and dynamic: the infant internalizes, at any given moment, both the mother's emergent as well as her continuous principle, along with the interaction between these two. In addition, the infant internalizes the interaction between the mother's continuous principle and his or her emergent (innate) one, as well as the interaction between the mother's emergent principle and the his or her continuous (innate) one.

Let us consider for a moment the ostensibly simple situation in which the mother holds and talks to her baby, who is making unhappy sounds. The part with which she tries to interpret her baby's "real" intention, will encourage the baby to form an impression about her continuous self – that is, about that part within the interaction that is in charge of the attempt to conceptualize reality in terms of causality and duration. A statement like: "when you made sounds like these yesterday you were hungry, so you must be hungry now" expresses the mother's attempt to relate to the infant's continuous self by referring to her own continuous self. Assuming that the baby is a stable and continuous entity that can be predicted and explained, she signals to the infant that she – a stable and continuous entity herself – also internalizes and remembers him or her as such. If these sounds signified hunger yesterday, then probably they do so today.

On the other hand, there are other statements, such as "I know, you're just too clever, you want to say something and you're angry because you can't . . .", which attribute something to the infant that is beyond his actual being and ability. The source of this kind of statement is in the mother's emergent self, which from the sounds the baby produces extracts a changing and new meaning. Such words are directed at the infant's emergent self because she credits him or her, too, with the ability to create new meaning and to want or dream beyond his or her actual existence.

Other interactions between the mother and the infant can also connect between the mother's continuous self and the infant's emergent self, as well as between the mother's emergent self and the infant's continuous self. All these interactions are dynamic and subject to change. Wherever the mother refuses to treat her baby in terms of causality, duration and meaning ("I haven't a clue what she wants. It's not as if one can even know the reason for this crying. She's got a different idea each time, it does not seem to connect to anything") – we can say that a malignant (or parasitic) interaction occurs (and is registered) between the mother's emergent self and the infant's continuous self. Forcing her emergent self on the continuous self of both the baby as well as her own and refusing to approach the baby as a continuous and stable entity, she invites him or her to enter an interaction that is psychotic in nature; one in which he or she cannot be contained, not even in the mother's mind and memory.

Elsewhere, when the mother insists to give a pure "realistic" interpretation to the baby's gurgles ("You must be either hungry, wet or tired. Whenever you cry, it is always because of one of these") she may be ignoring his or her emergent self as she imposes her rigid continuous self on the infant, as well as on her own perception: here she implies that her baby does not have the right to want something new, dream a dream that has not been dreamed before, desire something without knowing what it is. If every need the baby expresses is immediately filed under the general categories of what babies usually want or need, there is no room for creating a "singular baby", one who has a singular wish. There are, of course, also interactions that originate in the baby and his or her innate data. An over-sensitive baby may experience the mother's emergent self as violent and excessive, even if she presents it to him or her extremely gently, or else may experience her continuous self as rigid and suffocating rather than embracing, due to his or her thin psychic envelope.

As Bion argued (1962), the baby internalizes the mother not only as someone who has a "static knowledge" but also as someone who dynamically passes it on. This process of internalization is associated not only with the way in which the mother knows her child, but also with *how* she allows that child to know her. Here, too, there are many variations: a mother who is experienced by her child as allowing him to "know" or become familiar with her only in terms of the continuous self conveys an implicit message in which the child's emergent self features as destructive and dangerous. Such a mother is experienced as allowing her child to become familiar with her actual and objective features, while not allowing this child to *create* her in terms of his or her emergent self, or let him extract her potential, maybe unfulfilled, features.

One example that comes to my mind is a patient of mine, who in response to her four-year-old child's question, "aren't you the most beautiful, cleverest and strongest mother in the whole world?" answered: "well, I'm not all that beautiful and not particularly smart, actually and there are mothers who are much stronger than me." This mother's fear of her infant's emergent self, which was so eager to create her as omnipotent and perfect, caused her to wrap her child in a rigid, suffocating continuous self, encouraging him to stick closely to the solid and rigid boundaries of reality. An opposite example would probably be a mother who lets her child create her exclusively in terms of his or her emergent self, while ignoring the boundaries of her own continuous aspects, identifying with each and every projection to the point of losing her own outlines.

Since countless interactions between mother and infant occur at any given moment, as well as within the mother herself (and these inner interactions are internalized, too, by the infant), we never deal with one, isolated interaction or even a cluster of singular interactions as "a cause". Rather, the infant's psyche internalizes the sum total of recurrent and repeatedly internalized interactions, which pass through various levels of integration. Whenever a constructive interaction between the emergent and continuous occurs within the mother/child dyad, a certain level of integration is internalized, yielding a "lyrical feature". Each time a malignant interaction takes place, by contrast, integration is impaired so that the "lyrical feature" fails to evolve. But it is no less than the internalized sum total of these interactions, and its interaction with the child's inner and innate traits, that eventually determines the quality of the lyrical dimension and hence the quality of the potential space.

How does internalization of the emergent/continuous interaction within the primary dyad affect the development of the capacity for symbolization and reflection?

The capacity to symbolize, which constitutes the basis for the ability to reflect, is one of the most complex capacities of the human mind. The ability to create symbolic representations of external objects is a function of the ability to analyse and synthesize stimuli. Symbolization is grounded in the ability to perceive similarity between two elements, while also maintaining their distinct features. The aspect of the self responsible for perceiving similarity is the continuous self, which is responsible for perceiving each psychic detail as part of a continuum and of a whole. The emergent self, by contrast, has the capacity to identify and winnow whatever is singular, separate and distinct. The interaction between emergent and continuous enables the self to host the encounter between the capacity for discriminative analysis, as well as the capacity for synthesis. Whenever proper interaction between the emergent and the continuous principles is impossible, a proper capacity for symbolization will fail to arise, since the ability to identify what is common between elements – while also preserving their differences – did not evolve.

In the paranoid-schizoid position, as defined by Klein, the predominant mode of symbolization is one in which the symbol and the symbolized are not emotionally distinct, since an interpretive self that can negotiate between them is absent (see "Symbolic Equation", Segal, 1957). Experiencing oneself as an object and not as a subject, the individual at this stage does not attach meaning to one's own perceptions. Events are what they are and interpretation and perception are treated as identical processes (Ogden, 1986, p. 61). In such a situation, the person lacks a psychic vantage point. I believe that when there is no commensal interaction (and therefore no integration) between the emergent and the continuous within the primary dyad, the infant's psyche is not given the opportunity to constitute the lyrical vantage point that would allow it to look at its two facets – the emergent and the continuous – at one and the same time.

One of the derivatives of the interaction between the emergent and continuous self is the interaction between "me" and "not-me" data. It is into the deep-structure of the lyrical dimension, that is, into this very mould of the emergent/continuous internal as well as internalized interaction that "me" related data (i.e. the singular aspect of data that is the province of the emergent self) and "not-me" related data (i.e. the fixed and common aspect of data that is under the control of the continuous self) are poured. The quality of the integration of the "me" and the "not-me" related data in the primary dyad depends on the quality of integration of the emergent and the continuous. It is this integration that will, in the end, determine the transition from "being one" (a mother–baby unit in which the mother is perceived as a subjective object) to "being two" (the mother and baby as two separate objects), by means of connecting between the "me" and the "not-me", while also preserving their distinct features. Not less importantly, it will also enable the shift from "being two" to "being three": a mother, a child and an "interpretive subject" – that is, an onlooker who has the capacity to observe both the mother and him or herself.

I remarked earlier that the subject's ability to observe him or herself requires the existence of "a constant" that can serve as a kind of vantage point from which to observe "the ever-changing". The power of the dialectic between the emergent and the continuous is that each of these aspects both negates and validates the other simultaneously: since one only exists in relation to the other, without the former, the latter, too, will not exist. And thus the existence of a fixed and shared aspect provides the containing context to the changing and singular aspects, while, vice versa, the existence of the specific and mutable aspects fill this common context with meaning. The self's ability to grasp its own singularity follows from its ability to grasp itself as operating, as well, according to common rules. The lyrical dimension, which enables the containment of the singular self-perception within the perception of the self as operating according to common rules, is what enables the self to look at the specific from the vantage point of the general, at the mutable from the vantage point of the permanent, and at the unique from the vantage point of what is common and shared.

It is the distinction between the different qualities of the emergent and the continuous (which are preserved even within their integration) that forms the basis of the ability to distinguish between the symbol and the symbolized, namely between perception and interpretation. By making possible the integration between what is responsible for perception and what is responsible for interpretation, the lyrical dimension enables the existence of a perceiving and interpreting subject, one who has the capacity to own his or her symbols through rendering them meaningful.

If we reconsider this transition with reference to Klein's ideas, we can say that in the paranoid-schizoid position the symbol and symbolized are emotionally interchangeable, with the result of extreme concreteness of thought. When, however, symbol and symbolized become distinguishable, a sense of I-ness fills the hiatus between them. The interpreting "I" mediates between one's thought and that which one is thinking about; between the self and one's sensory experience. As soon as the infant experiences itself as the interpreter of his experience – he as a subject is born. From this moment on each experience is a personal creation.

Hence, while in the paranoid-schizoid position, everything is what it is – in the depressive position each event is what the individual makes of it (Ogden, 1986, pp. 72–73). Giving up omnipotence and acknowledging the separateness of the other and his or her existence beyond one's control – both characteristic features of the depressive position – means that the symbolized (the real object, the referent of one's thoughts) is freed from the symbol that one has created (Ogden, 1986, pp. 76–77). The space that now opens between the individual's omnipotence and what exists outside and beyond this omnipotence is, in fact, the potential space. It is not only by means of the distinction between symbol and symbolized or between perception and interpretation that the lyrical dimension constitutes the potential space, but also through the integration between them which makes it possible to preserve their individual features while at the same time joining together the various aspects that they represent in human experience.

Ogden (1986) relates to the mechanism of splitting (in the context of the schizoid-paranoid position) as causing historical discontinuity, arguing that it re-writes history from scratch again and again, adjusting it to the present. As a result, the past is constantly changing: each new event changes all previous ones. The present is immediately projected onto all previous experiences, thus annihilating the past. This creates a frozen timeless present, inaccessible to reflection (p. 80). In a state of mind where splitting processes take over, there is neither experience of continuity, nor can a person experience him or herself as the same person through different emotional states:

> Basic to the state of being characterizing the paranoid-schizoid position is the continual rewriting of history in the service of maintaining discontinuities of loving and hating aspects of self and object. It is essential that only one emotional plane exists at a time. Otherwise, object relations become contaminated and, as a result, unbearably complex for the primitive psyche.
>
> *(Ogden, 1986, p. 65)*

As explained earlier, the experience of incessant changing, which is the result of the discontinuity between the different emotional planes, turns the emotional experience into one that is not available for reflection. In the absence of a constant that exists beyond change, it is impossible to perceive changes. The lyrical dimension, which is in charge of the integration of the constant with the changeable as well as of the experience of "me" and "not-me", supplies, in fact, the psyche's centre of gravity, which stays constant and stable beyond fluctuations. Thus, due to its stability, it makes those very fluctuations possible. The lyrical dimension, it could be said, is responsible for the experience of selfhood beyond the specific "self-data", that is, for the deep experience of a continuous and stable self over and beyond the changes through which this self passes at any given point in time.

It is only reasonable to assume that, in addition to being vital to the formation of the potential space in Winnicott's terms, the lyrical dimension is also crucial to the shift between the schizoid-paranoid position and the depressive position in Klein's terms. The experience of continuous selfhood requires an ability of self reflection. Humans are the one species that are able, by means of self-contemplation and over and beyond all changes, to remember who they were in the past, and hence, also realize who they are in the present. In contrast to what occurs in the paranoid-schizoid position (prior to the formation of subjectivity and to the stable formation of a lyrical dimension), within which the past keeps changing constantly and every new contingency re-writes whatever has happened before – it is in the depressive position that the infant starts experiencing both him or herself as well as the other as having a continuous and chronological existence. The more constructive interactions between the emergent and the continuous accrue, and the more moments of integration between them – the greater are the chances that the person will move from a schizoid-paranoid mode to one informed by the depressive position and will become capable of subjectivity, of processes of mourning, and of an experience of continuity, memory and compassion.

What is the connection between the capacity for dialectics, reflection and symbolization – and the function of creating meaning?

The capacity for dialectics is the capacity to shift between "me" and "not-me". Based on the latter, the capacity to symbolize is the capacity to represent "me-data" in terms of "not-me". Finally, based on the capacity for symbolization, the capacity to reflect consists of the capacity to render "not-me" related data meaningful in terms of the "me" experience, namely to identify, within the general data, the singular meaning given them by the context of selfhood.

There is a huge difference between *attributing* self-related meaning to non-self related data, and, by contrast, *projecting* self-related meaning onto non–self-related data. The difference inheres in the fact that while projection imposes internal meaning onto an external reality – namely identifies the external reality with the internal one – the attribution of self-related meaning to non-self-related data is based on a distinction between inside and outside. The result of this distinction is an ability to release the singular from the common, the private from the general: our ability to understand that within the "red" that can be perceived by every eye there is always enfolded the inner hue which is born of the fusion between the external colour and one's own gaze.

The process that consists of the movement (by means of dialectics) between outside and inside, of the ability to represent (through symbolization) the internal in external terms, and of the ability (through reflection) to identify the internal within the external is precisely the process of creating meaning. While this process is not one of creation pure and simple, it does not consist of mere extraction either. It is located somewhere in between these two. The process of "extracting meaning", in fact, always includes an element of creation or generation since in it the psyche serves, simultaneously, as a "midwife" of meaning (by means of the lyrical dimension), as the womb that "gives birth" to meaning (namely the self) and as the newborn itself (the experience of selfhood).

At each and every moment, whenever integration between the emergent and the continuous occurs and a lyrical dimension, instituting meaning, arises – another layer of self comes into being and thus further deepens and stabilizes it. The process by which meaning is created is, in fact, the very process of psychic birth.

Note

1 This conceptualization coheres both with Bion's (1962) thinking about the mother–infant relation as a container/contained interaction and with Grotstein's (2000) description of the mother's face as a screen onto which either the infant's dream or the infant-as-dream is projected.

References

Bion, W.R. (1962). *Learning from Experience*. London: Heinemann. [Reprinted London: Karnac Books, 1984.]

Grotstein, J.S. (2000). *Who Is the Dreamer Who Dreams the Dream?* New Jersey and London: The Analytic Press.

Ogden, T. (1986). *The Matrix of the Mind*. Northvale, NJ; London: Jason Aronson.

Segal, H. (1957). Notes on Symbol Formation. *International Journal of Psycho-Analysis*, 38, pp. 391–397.

5

ASLEEP WITH ALL FIVE SENSES AWAKE

Octavio Paz's "As One Listens to the Rain" as an illustration of the interrelations between the emergent and the continuous principles of the self

As One Listens to the Rain[1]

> Listen to me as one listens to the rain,
> not attentive, not distracted,
> light footsteps, thin drizzle,
> water that is air, air that is time,
> the day is still leaving,
> the night has yet to arrive,
> figurations of mist
> at the turn of the corner,
> figurations of time
> at the bend in this pause,
> listen to me as one listens to the rain,
> without listening, hear what I say
> with eyes open inward, asleep
> with all five senses awake,
> it's raining, light footsteps, a murmur of syllables,
> air and water, words with no weight:
> what we are and are,
> the days and years, this moment,
> weightless time and heavy sorrow,
> listen to me as one listens to the rain,
> wet asphalt is shining,
> steam rises and walks away,
> night unfolds and looks at me,
> you are you and your body of steam,
> you and your face of night,

you and your hair, unhurried lightning,
you cross the street and enter my forehead,
footsteps of water across my eyes,
listen to me as one listens to the rain,
the asphalt's shining, you cross the street,
it is the mist, wandering in the night,
it is the night, asleep in your bed,
it is the surge of waves in your breath,
your fingers of water dampen my forehead,
your fingers of flame burn my eyes,
your fingers of air open eyelids of time,
a spring of visions and resurrections,
listen to me as one listens to the rain,
the years go by, the moments return,
do you hear the footsteps in the next room?
not here, not there: you hear them
in another time that is now,
listen to the footsteps of time,
inventor of places with no weight, nowhere,
listen to the rain running over the terrace,
the night is now more night in the grove,
lightning has nestled among the leaves,
a restless garden adrift-go in,
your shadow covers this page.

"Listen to me as one listens to the rain," (1) (Paz, 1987) says the poet, and explains: "not attentive, not distracted," (2) that is, neither intent on me as if I were a completely external object, nor wholly immersed in your own internal world. "As one listens to the rain," namely situating the object in-between inside and out, in-between what demands our attention and what forms the background to our attention to ourselves. Paz continues: "water that is air, air that is time,/the day is still leaving" (4–5). This cycle in which water evaporates into air which turns into time – the same psychic cycle in which motion is not only upward and ahead but also inward, into the deep interchanging essence of things – is also at the very foundation of our ability to overcome time, or to overcome time-imposed absurdity. "The day is still leaving": the ability to touch the essence of things – fixed yet constantly changing – is at the very root of our ability to exist beyond timelessness, or to touch upon the eternal.

"Figurations of mist/at the turn of the corner," (7–8) he goes on, "figurations of time/at the bend in this pause" (9–10). To what could "the bend in this pause" be referring? This, I believe, is the very fold in time that emerges in the potential space through the workings of the lyrical dimension. It is not about stopping time but rather about an attempt to divert it from the linear axis proceeding from birth to death – into a space in which the psyche may move not only forward but inward. The ability to turn inward, or to transform the planar movement into one within a three-dimensional space, creates a fold in time by allowing the psyche zones in which it is possible to let go of the knowledge of finitude and experience eternity and boundlessness.

> listen to me as one listens to the rain,
> without listening, hear what I say
> with eyes open inward, asleep
> with all five senses awake
> *(Paz, 1987, 11–14)*

Paz, here, directs us to that precious zone of attention which, while being focused neither exclusively outward nor exclusively inward, combines both these modes, attending to the way the external is reconfigured in the psychic interiority. The ability to hear the other's voice without hearing him as an "other"; that is, to hear him with eyes opened inward, reflects the ability to create a psychic space in which one can perceive oneself as well as the other both from the inside, as a kind of "self", and from the outside, as a kind of other.

Paz's condensed poetic expression shows us that listening is not a two-dimensional act that includes the mere passing of information from one's mouth to the other's ear, but one that takes place in three dimensions – namely in a space in which the experience of self and the experience of the other are not polar opposites but constitute two superimposed aspects of experience, thereby creating an effect of depth. "[A] sleep with all five senses awake" (14) – thus preserving the freedom to dream while at the same time maintaining the ability to wholly address oneself outward.

"What we were and are,/the days and years, this moment" (17–18): the lyrical dimension of the potential space makes it possible for us to linger in an eternal present. One that holds both past and future, the continuous order of things and the chronological flow of details, along with a sense of uniqueness and freshness: both of the moment and of us being in that moment.

"Night unfolds and looks at me" (23): in other words: it is not just that we look at what stands outside us, but what stands outside us also looks at us. This, in fact, is nothing but another way of pointing out the simultaneity of the experience of self and other, and the complex mobility of the psychic gaze. It is not just the listening that is not a planar action: looking isn't planar as well. In the process of listening, things are conveyed simultaneously in both directions, inward and out, and the same is true for the process of looking. In that sense, any perceptual event involves, beyond the reciprocal movement between "me" and "not-me", a simultaneous experience of the world outside oneself, which allows *looking at it* – as well as an experience of the world as existing within oneself, making it possible *to look at oneself through it*.

"You cross the street and enter my forehead" (27). Is this just a poetic way of describing the manner in which external objects insert themselves into our thoughts? Or might it refer to what I earlier mentioned when discussing the "possible" enfolded within the "actual" (Gilead, 1999, 2003)? When the addressee of these lines crosses the street and enters the poet's forehead, she in fact turns from being an actual object into a possible one. Crossing the street releases her possibilities, and in that sense calls her to enter a sphere beyond her actual existence. This integration between the actual space and the possible space indeed offers her a far more extensive, rich and timeless existence:

> it is the night, asleep in your bed,
> it is the surge of waves in your breath,
> [. . .] your fingers of air open eyelids of time,
> a spring of visions and resurrections
> > *(Paz, 1987, 32–33, 36–37)*

"A spring of visions and resurrections" (37); that is, the ability to see time coming to life again and again, and in that way turning into timelessness.

> Do you hear the footsteps in the next room?
> not here, not there: you hear them
> in another time that is now
> > *(Paz, 1987, 40–43)*

The ability to hear the footsteps in another place (the next room) and in "another time" implies the ability to be "not here, not there"; to exist, that is, in the interstices between the actual "here" and the possible "there". This in-between space contains "another time that is now": an experience of time that does not rely on the chronological order of facts, but on the latter's location in a context of meaning that transforms our current existence into something sui generis. This "another time" is the pause or hiatus that allows for our singular existence within the general time. It is, in this sense, not quite time as such, but rather a psychic space: "Listen to the footsteps of time,/inventor of places with no weight, nowhere" (44–45). Within the psyche, time is actually a place: not an actual place, but rather the possibility of a place that is weightless – and yet contains the entire psychic motion.

Paz concludes:

> Listen to the rain running over the terrace,
> the night is now more night in the grove,
> lightning has nestled among the leaves,
> a restless garden adrift-go in,
> your shadow covers this page.
> > *(Paz, 1987, 46–50)*

The one caesura in this poem's flow – written almost as one unbroken sentence – occurs between "a restless garden adrift" and "come, your shadow covers this page". Perhaps because the endless movement between outside and inside creates a "restless garden" in the psyche – a blurred space lacking boundaries between "me" and "not-me". Perhaps because what circumscribes the movement, and in the end allows us "to see", is the shadow of the object that falls on our blank page. What allows the indistinct unit of "me"/"not-me" to become a distinct condition in which the existence of object, subject and subjectivity becomes possible – is the existence of a distinct object, ready to be assimilated by the self, while nevertheless preserving its own matchless outline.

Beyond announcing her actual existence, the shadow of the poem's addressee also enables the existence of the metaphorical page. It enables the possible zone in the poet's mind within which things can be experienced and written.

Note

1 By Octavio Paz, from *The Collected Poems, 1957–1987* reprinted by permission of Pollinger Limited (www.pollingerltd.com) on behalf of the Estate of Octavio Paz.

References

Gilead, A. (1999). *Saving Possibilities: A Study in Philosophical Psychology*. Amsterdam: Rodopi.

Gilead, A. (2003). How Does Love Make the Ugly Beautiful? *Philosophy and Literature*, 27(2), pp. 436–443.

Paz, Octavio. (1987). *The Collected Poems of Octavio Paz, 1957–1987: Bilingual Edition*. Ed. Eliot Weinberger. New York: New Directions Books.

6

THE INFLUENCE OF THE CONTINUOUS/EMERGENT INTERACTION ON THE DEVELOPMENT OF SCHIZOID AND BORDERLINE PERSONALITIES

In the five previous chapters I dealt with the manner in which the lyrical dimension constitutes the potential space and the capacity for dialectics, symbolization and reflection. Now I would like to direct my attention to how, within the relations of the infant and the primary object, inappropriate internalizations of the emergent and the continuous may generate a "malignant containment", which impairs the formation of the lyrical dimension and, thus, of the potential space. Two kinds of mental organization represent, in this context, the polar extremes of psychopathology (this polarity does not reflect their severity but their antithetical nature): the schizoid personality and the borderline personality.

The schizoid personality

When discussing the schizoid personality, Wilfred Bion's important notion of the mother as a knowing and knowledge-imparting object (1962a) forms an interesting point of departure. The baby's attempts to "know" the mother generates, according to Bion, one's primary template for knowing both oneself and the world. Through the interaction with the mother, the infant internalizes a knowing and knowledge-imparting object. A person who internalizes such an object, Bion argues, will be capable of self-knowledge and of communicating between various aspects of him or herself, as well as reflecting about oneself. A mother who is experienced by her child as being hostile towards any attempt at projective identification actually offers the child a sense of a world that does not want to know him and does not want to be known by him either. For this child, any type of integration will be an unbearable menace (Bion, 1962a). Since we can consider the continuous and the emergent as types of perception, and therefore as types of knowledge, I would like to suggest a re-reading of Bion's argument with reference to the notions of the continuous self, the emergent self and their interaction.

The pathological mother, argues Bion, is a mother who does not let her child "know" her. What does Bion mean by "knowing"? I don't believe that what he meant was a simple acquaintance of the maternal object, but rather a much more complicated type of knowing. What I would like to suggest is that the mother who supposedly does not let her child "know" her is in fact a mother who does not allow her child to "create" her, but only to become familiar with her. In my terms, this is a mother who does not allow her child to know her in terms of the emergent self, but only in terms of the continuous self. Such a mother is perceived by her child as inviting him or her to get to know her objective actual figure – that is, her figure as the child's continuous self perceives it – but won't allow her child entrance to her "Behind the Scenes" rich subjectivity, and all the more so – won't let his or her emergent subjectivity to "create" her. In other words, she can cope with her child's knowing her in terms of the shared reality, but not with the possibility of her being subjected to the child's omnipotent control within the realm of his or her emergent self. This inability leaves her reduced and sterile in the child's experience.

Accordingly, the child may also experience him or herself, as well as the external world, as sterile and reduced. This kind of child may therefore internalize a persecutory and rigid continuous principle and an impotent and lifeless emergent principle. Using the familiar terms of psychopathology, this interaction will result in a personality structure with schizoid features, within which any zone dominated by the emergent self (such as love relations, creative work, or even dream work) might turn lifeless. Such a person will avoid social situations or interactions involving emotional intensity, and will be perceived as remote and disconnected. Since giving free reign to the emergent self is attended by a sense of danger, he or she will keep it reduced to an extreme degree, keeping it out of anyone's as well as one's own sight. This psychic state, in fact, resembles the computer's "safe mode": a state of extremely limited functioning that prevents collapse of the entire system.

In his major paper, "Schizoid Factors in the Personality" (1940), Fairbairn points out how, in the schizoid personality, the ability to take dominates over the ability to give. Giving – which includes the capacity to express feelings to an other – is associated in the schizoid's experience with the loss of bodily contents; something that leads to experiencing every interaction as exhausting. Formulating this in terms of the continuous and the emergent self, the schizoid person's problem is in revealing his or her unique psychic contents, which is to say, in being in touch with the contents of his or her emergent self. Fairbairn assumes that what I call the emergent principle may be present as a potential in the schizoid psyche, and can even be developed to some extent, yet it is unable to express itself in relations with either an object or even with the self as a type of object (i.e. in a way that involves a degree of reflectiveness and self-consciousness). As mentioned, a mother who is perceived by her child as referring to the child's emergent self as dangerous might raise a child who experiences his own emergent self, in every respect, as potentially destructive; not just towards external objects, but also with regard to the foundations of objective perception, i.e. with regard to the continuous principle within him or herself.

The tragedy of the schizoid person, according to Fairbairn, is that, in the former's experience, it is not his hatred that does the damage but his love. He therefore keeps his love not just in a safe box (as a precious object) but in a locked cage, as he believes it is too dangerous to be at large in the open world of objects. At one and the same time, the schizoid person experiences his or her emergent self as a precious, extremely fragile treasure, and as a ticking bomb. The merest wrong touch will irreversibly destroy the fragile core, causing it to explode and to annihilate, along with it, the continuous self including all its internal and external representations. We must remember that the schizoid person's continuous self has persecutory and rigid qualities, and is extremely fragile. As a result, even a minor expression of the emergent self will become a source of danger.

In the therapeutic relationship, therefore, the therapist or analyst will often experience the schizoid patient as hyper-reactive to the tiniest of emotional stimuli. Where containment of the emergent by the continuous is impossible, survival requires the curbing of all expressions of the emergent in order to avoid the flooding of the entire intra-psychic space. The emergent self, whose essence lies in creating every object anew at each moment, is experienced as destructive, since through its wish to recreate it may actually demolish the created object. In fact, the attack that the continuous principle wages on the schizoid person's emergent principle is related to the former's desperate attempt to prevent what it experiences as a suicidal attack that may eventually bring down both the emergent and the continuous.

Fairbairn originally presented this as the mode of interrelating with external objects that is typical of the schizoid person. I would like to draw attention to the great relevance, too, of these arguments to the internal and internalized psychic interactions. As mentioned, a child who has experienced a "malignant" interaction both between his or her emergent principle and the continuous principle represented by the maternal object, as well as between the maternal own emergent and continuous principles, will probably adopt the same malignant pattern of interaction in everything implying the relations between the emergent and the continuous principles within his or her own self. Since the continuous principle was internalized in this case as persecutory, rigid and fragile, any attempted interaction on the part of the emergent principle will be experienced as an internal attack or as an attack on interiority, which must be avoided at all cost.

Britton's (1998) notion of "malignant containment" refers to the situation in which one element of the self attacks the other with the result that the entire psychic immune system comes under risk of collapse. Where there is a malignant interaction, no integration between the two mutually attacking elements is possible. In the absence of a third dimension that allows their co-existence, the self is left to oscillate between two split poles. Indeed, this two-dimensionality is very typical of the analytic experience with schizoid patients, which is often characterized by the feeling that a space allowing for transference or symbolic interpretations fails to come into existence, much like the patient expresses no interest whatsoever in gaining any understanding of his or her inner world.

In parallel to the schizoid external relations as well as to the schizoid internal relations, psychotherapy or psychoanalysis, too, takes place on a concrete plane (rather than in a space) that enables analysis but not synthesis, since it allows the coexistence of elements side by side but not their mutual containment. Thus, for instance, a schizoid patient, whose last therapeutic session had ended in great tension, answered his analyst's question as to how he'd coped coming in by saying – "I came in my car". He clearly could not understand the symbolic aspect of this question – relating to his psychic reality and to his feelings towards the previous meeting – and was able to respond to its concrete sense only. He had not come in "with difficulty", or "easily", or "worried" or "with a sense of relief". He had come "in his car". Impairment of the lyrical dimension comes, for the schizoid person, at the price of leading an existence of survival only, without any sense of vitality and desire. Locked in his or her bare psychic space, the schizoid person remains in a world in which acts take the place of feelings and facts come instead of the ability to fantasize and dream.

In his book *The Primitive Edge of Experience*, Thomas Ogden describes schizoid emptiness as follows:

> The schizoid patient is "occupied by", and preoccupied with, his internal object relationships; and yet these relationships are, in themselves, insubstantial, leading to a state of emotional impoverishment. The situation is analogous to that of the infant suffering from merycism in which the same food is swallowed, regurgitated, and re-swallowed again and again. In this process, the food is depleted of its nutritive value and eventually the infant may starve to death despite the fact that his mouth and stomach are regularly full.
>
> *(Ogden, 1989, p. 86)*

What Ogden means by "schizoid object relations" is the schizoid person's withdrawal from object relations into an internal world consisting of conscious and unconscious relations with internal objects. As a result, the schizoid person remains trapped in his or her inner drama, experiencing senselessness and emptiness. Formulating schizoid withdrawal in terms of the dynamics presented above, we may say that the schizoid person's experience of his or her emergent self is so destructive and demanding that he or she suppresses it by "voiding" all objects – both internal and external – of their emergent aspect: "These phantasied object relations are conducted in a realm of omnipotent thought with heavy reliance on splitting and projective identification as modes of defense" (Ogden, 1989, p. 85). This splitting can also be formulated as a splitting between the emergent and the continuous self, while omnipotence can be conceived as finding expression in the wish to "void" the emergent in order to safeguard the existence of the self. However, the emergent can never be fully evacuated from the self. It goes on to exist as an isolated, inaccessible capsule that holds vitality, while the surface of the self, the part that encounters the outer world, is left sterile, empty and lifeless.

The schizoid person, in fact, does not retreat into the inner world from object relations, but rather withdraws his or her inner world in order to survive object relations. In other words, the schizoid person takes his or her emergent self into hiding in order to prevent it from endangering the existence of the continuous self and the ongoing existence of his or her significant objects. Fasting is better than suffocation, since it holds the possibility of reparation. Resonating Winnicott's notion of the "false self" (1960), one may say that the schizoid person believes it is better to keep the emergent core under lock and in isolation than to expose it to daylight and allow it to nullify the continuous or allow the continuous to identify and annihilate the emergent. The schizoid solution, therefore, is to turn from living to surviving: the emergent self, which is in charge of the sense of vitality, becomes frozen and detached so as to allow the continuous self, which is in charge of the sense of reality, to keep the functional shell intact and unmarred.

In a chapter dedicated to the psychopathology of the potential space in *The Matrix of the Mind* (1986), Ogden presents four distinct forms of failure to create or adequately maintain the dialectical psychological process. The first is *the collapse of the dialectic of reality and fantasy in the direction of fantasy* (in which reality is subsumed by fantasy and the latter turns into a thing in itself); the second is *the dialectic of reality and fantasy collapsing in the direction of reality* (where reality comes to serve as a defense against fantasy); the third is *the dissociation between reality and fantasy* (where like in fetishism, a splitting in the ego occurs in order to avoid specific meaning), and the fourth failure of the psychic dialectic takes the form of a cessation of the attribution of meaning to perception, namely a state in which *neither reality nor fantasy can be created* (Ogden, 1986, pp. 215–216).

It seems to me that it is the second of these categories that fits the schizoid personality. Reframing it in this book's terms: the failure in creating and maintaining the dialectic between the emergent and the continuous elements triggers the failure to create the lyrical dimension of the psyche, and hence to constitute a potential space. As a result, the interaction between the emergent and the continuous turns into a malignant containment, one in which the continuous principle suffocates the emergent principle, reducing it to a bare minimum. Since the lyrical dimension is constitutive of the potential space, the potential space that results in this case is of an extremely poor quality, or does not come into existence at all.

The impaired formation of the potential space of the schizoid personality is reflected in deficiencies in all three abovementioned functions: the dialectic between inside and outside, the capacity for symbolization and the capacity for reflection. The schizoid person's inability to simultaneously hold on to both the "me" and the "not-me" data and to shift between them; his or her inability to represent the "me" data in terms of the "not-me", and finally his or her inability to render the "not-me" data meaningful in terms of the self – all interfere with the ability to create meaning, that is to say, to give birth to the singular combination of traits that is unique to his or her specific personality.

The meaning of the *collapse into reality* here is that the schizoid person will function normally as long as functioning requires movement on a two-dimensional surface level rather than in three-dimensional space. When the latter must be taken into account, however, the schizoid person will resemble someone that lacks a sense of depth but is expected to make sense of perspective. In terms of the potential space, such a person will be able to move from the stage of "being one" to that of "being two" (mother and infants as objects), but not from "being two" to "being three" – the level at which one exists as a subject who can observe oneself as well as the (m)other while being able to infuse one's symbols with personal meaning. And indeed, Ogden argues in this context that when what he calls the "reality pole of the dialectical process" is used predominantly as a defense against fantasy, the price is the foreclosure of imagination. Here is his illustration:

> When a relatively unrestricted psychological dialectical process has been established, a little girl playing house is both a little girl and a mother, and the question of which she is, never arises. Being a little girl who feels loved by her mother (*in reality*) makes it safe for her to borrow what is her mother's (in *fantasy*) without fear of retaliation or fear of losing herself in her mother, and, as a result, disappearing as a separate person. Being a mother (in *fantasy*) gives the little girl access to and use of all the richness of the cultural, familial and personal symbols (e.g., in relation to what it means to be a female, a mother, and a daughter) that have been consciously and unconsciously conveyed in the course of *real* experience with her mother, father, and others.
>
> On the other hand, if the little girl is *only* a little girl, she is unable to play; she is unable to imagine and will be unable to feel she is alive in any full sense. Such a situation arises when reality must be used as a defense against fantasy.
>
> *(Ogden, 1986, pp. 219–220)*

Ogden then goes on to argue that patients who chronically experience this form of collapse of the dialectical process hardly ever present dreams. In other words: their dreams are hardly distinguishable from their conscious thoughts, and often their dream associations, too, come in the form of a cataloguing in terms of which parts of the dream did or did not "really" occur. Trying to find personal significance in the observed details, Ogden writes, is "like trying to get blood from a stone" (p. 221). The fixity of the patient's focus on reality is designed to "drain the blood out" of fantasy, keeping it squeaky clean, while the expropriation of the dialectic resonance between fantastic and realistic leaves the schizoid person robbed of any ability to imagine (Ogden, 1986, p. 221).

According to Ogden, the *collapse into reality* happens as a result of fantasy being too "close" to reality – therefore constituting a threat. When fantasy may turn into reality, it becomes a force that can endanger that reality. Sticking close to reality and avoiding fantasy is in fact a defense against the feeling that fantasy might take over reality and merge with it. My earlier explanation of the development of the schizoid personality agrees with this description. Since the emergent is perceived as an armed robber who infiltrates the unprotected public space,[1] it is up to the continuous to keep it reined as much as possible so as to safeguard the latter's boundaries.

This struggle between the forces of reality and fantasy actually derives from the primary struggle between the continuous and the emergent in the psyche. It is not about the dichotomy between reality and fantasy, but about a more fundamental division which actually runs across each of these categories as such. Not reality struggling against fantasy, but rather the continuous elements of the person's sense of reality, as well as those of his fantasy and of the inter-subjective interaction between self and other – struggling against the emergent aspects of these categories.

To illustrate a clinical process of this type, Ogden describes the case of a boy who was allowed to witness his parents during sexual intercourse, as well as the very painful delivery of his younger brother. He developed an exaggerated tendency to keep close to the exact constituents of reality and steered clear of any use of his imagination or fantasy. Ogden (1986, pp. 220-221) argues that since the danger of this boy's wishes and fears "coming true" was too real, he reacted by avoiding contact with them. I would argue that early exposure to the possibility of fantasy becoming reality does not suffice to explain the mechanism of *collapse into reality*. We may equally claim that this boy was likely to develop something resembling a borderline personality: having experienced reality as undifferentiated from fantasy, he would continue using materials deriving from fantasy as though they were reality-related materials.

The difference between the schizoid and the borderline solution to the described situation is the character of the internalized continuous, of the internalized emergent, and of the internalized interaction between them. By this I mean both the interaction within the child's self and that in the inter-subjective space between the mother and child. If in the internalized interaction the continuous reduces the emergent, the described events will issue in a *collapse into reality*. If, however, in the internalized interaction the emergent actually overpowers the continuous, the result of the same events will be a *collapse into fantasy*. It is the internalized interaction between emergent and continuous that forms the basis of the self's tendency towards one structural solution rather than another.

The borderline personality disorder

In the borderline structure of personality – unlike in the development of the schizoid personality structure – the child internalizes an object whose boundaries are weak, one who is experienced as symbiotic and non-distinct. The non-separateness of the object turns the infant's experience into one in which the emergent principle is not contained by a stable continuous object but takes the upper hand over the object's continuous aspects while crushing its boundaries. As a result, the child internalizes a confused sense of inside and outside, with a priority of the former over the latter and hence also over the reality principle. This constitutes the groundwork for the psychotic slippages that characterize the "low level" type of the borderline personality structure.

Here, too, the lyrical dimension of the potential space is damaged. But the damage is of a different kind: in the absence of a stable border that may contain change, the world is internalized as constantly changing. When the emergent and the continuous are indistinguishable, reality testing is affected and with it the ability to recognize the other as separate while simultaneously experiencing that other as available to intimacy and love. This internalized pathological interaction between the continuous and the emergent explains the fluctuation typical of borderline patients who tend to keep shifting between idealization and devaluation of any object, thereby maintaining an extreme splitting between good and evil (Kernberg, 1967). This fluctuation is related to a lack of context that may contain good and evil, which is one of the consequences of the absent capacity for dialectic and integration. In that way, the world is experienced as a surface that can only be examined by means of an oscillation between its one extreme and the other, with no possibility to envelop it in one overarching view, or to experience it as simultaneously having volume and boundaries.

The borderline personality is characterized by a great difficulty in regulating emotions and impulses. This is not surprising if we remember that the child, in this case, has internalized a destructive interaction pattern in which the emergent prevails over the continuous, preventing it from either containing or regulating the former. As a result of this internalized interaction pattern, the infant's emergent self engages in an ongoing onslaught against the boundaries of the continuous self, which becomes weaker and weaker. The great abandonment anxiety, which is characteristic of the borderline personality, results from the experience that the borderline person actually "destroys" the object each time he or she "creates" it – that is, whenever his or her emergent principle comes into contact with the continuous principle of the other, or with the continuous principle *as an-other*. The sense of annihilation is linked not only to every contact with an external object, but also to every objective perception of the world and of him or herself.

Since the internalized primary object is an ever-changing one, an object that does not maintain stable and fixed outlines either, the child experiences him or herself as intrusive and destructive. *Thus, the early generative experience of the creation of the world turns into an experience of returning chaos.* This kind of inversion will accompany every act of psychic creativity from now on, as well as love relations and friendships. This constant takeover of the continuous by the emergent within the self (which is the internalized representation of the relations between the infant and its primary object) also serves to explain how the borderline personality slips into psychotic states, during which recognition of the laws of a common reality vanishes almost completely, while the world is created over and over again in terms of the emergent self with no possibility of containing it within any kind of continuous principle. As a result, all parts of the continuous self are expropriated, including the ability for causal thinking and for temporal and spatial perception. In cases of acute psychosis, characterizing *low-organization* type of borderline personalities (Kernberg, 1967), the person indeed loses his or her sense of orientation in space and time, while his or her grasp of the reasons for this condition is harmed by lack of judgement and extreme idiosyncrasy.

I shall try now to examine the formation of the potential space in the borderline personality structure in terms of the interaction between the continuous self and the emergent self. If previously I suggested that the characteristic interaction between emergent and continuous in the schizoid personality structure (an interaction during which the continuous stifles the emergent) does not allow the transition from "being two" to "being three", I would presently like to suggest that the continuous/ emergent interaction typical of the borderline personality structure (one in which the emergent "undoes" the boundaries of the continuous), allows not even the shift from "being one" to "being two" (let alone from "being two" to "being three").

The manner in which the emergent prevails over the continuous in the primary mother–infant unit does not, in fact, allow for processes of separation. Since the emergent (infant) is breaching and annulling the boundaries of the continuous (object), the infant misses the opportunity to encounter the paradox in which mother and child are one and simultaneously two. During the phase of complete object relatedness, which occurs after the environmental mother has been internalized, the infant moves from the process of *creating* the mother to that of *discovering* her. The further progress of his or her development, that is to say, his or her ability to use the object (Winnicott, 1967) and to develop a psychological space, depends on the mother's ability to survive as an external object over time. In this context Winnicott states that the fact that the baby destroys the maternal object while the maternal object survives this onslaught, is exactly what allows the baby to discover externality, namely the reassuring fact that the mother exists beyond his or her control (*ibid.*).

When, however, the baby's experience is that the external object evaporates and its outlines alter according to the projections of his or her emergent self, that is to say – the object identifies with the baby's projections – the infant will experience him or herself as having been given permission to destroy the object. A mother who wholly identifies with her child's projections prevents this child from discovering her externality. In doing so, she also prevents him or her from internalizing a continuous self that will serve as a reliable container for the emergent self. This leads, within the infant's psyche, to the destruction not only of the object but also of objectivity, thus to the incapacity to internalize a constructive interaction in which the emergent is contained by the continuous without the annihilation of the continuous boundaries. This can be rephrased in Ogden's (1986, pp. 215–216) terms as a situation in which impairment in the formation of the potential space (as a result of the impairment in the formation of a lyrical dimension) brings about *a collapse in the direction of fantasy*, where reality is subsumed by fantasy and the latter turns into a thing in itself.

"When the reality pole of the psychological dialectic collapses, the subject becomes tightly imprisoned in the realm of fantasy objects as things in themselves", argues Ogden (*ibid.*, p. 216). This is a two-dimensional world, experienced as a collection of facts. To people with this experience, delusion does not sound like a voice but is, itself, a voice. This also constitutes the basis for the delusional transference (Little, 1958; Searles, 1963) in which the analyst is not "like" the patient's mother – but actually *is* the patient's mother. When nothing represents anything but itself, then only very little of what a person experiences is understandable.

Understanding, says Ogden, involves a layering of meanings in which one layer forms the context from which the others derive their significance. Where there is an inability to distinguish between the symbol and the symbolized, whatever is perceived is not mediated by subjectivity; that is, by a sense of oneself as the creator of meanings. Perceptions, then, carry an impersonal imperative for action and therefore must be gotten rid of, or clung to, or be put into someone else, and so on. What the person is unable to do, according to Ogden, is to understand. Since there is no space between symbol and symbolized, the interpretation and the external event that is interpreted are treated as if they were one. There is no room in which ideas and emotions can be entertained. Illusion turns into delusion, thoughts become plans, feelings become actions. Understanding the meaning of one's experience is only possible when one thing can *stand for* an other without *being* that other. This is what constitutes the capacity for symbol formation, a capacity that frees the individual from the prison of the "thing in itself" (Ogden, 1986, pp. 218–219).

In Bion's terms (1962), this situation can be described as one in which instead of the mother containing the infant's projected contents in her *reverie*, so that she can return them processed and tolerable, she actually becomes those projections. In the absence of a stable enough continuous principle that will contain the infantile emergent principle within the mother–baby unit, the continuous becomes *the reflection of the emergent*. This renders the containment of the emergent by the continuous a malignant one. It is this impairment of the lyrical dimension, and hence also of the potential space, that forms the groundwork of the borderline personality structure. It explains the tendency of people with this type of personality structure to confuse reality and imagination; it explains their difficulty in creating a symbolic space, their shifts between the omnipotent pole and the impotent pole, as well as their abandonment anxiety, which is associated with their experience of themselves as destroying both object and objectivity.

Note

1 The public, in this context, represents the role of the continuous as responsible for the "public" and common components of the psyche; with the emergent, by contrast, being in charge of the "personal" and private.

References

Bion, W.R. (1962). The Psycho-Analytic Study of Thinking. *International Journal of Psycho-Analysis*, 43, pp. 306–310.

Bion, W.R. (1962a). *Learning from Experience*. London: Heinemann. [Reprinted London: Karnac Books, 1984.]

Britton, R. (1998). Naming and Containing. In *Belief and Imagination*. London: Routledge, in association with the Institute of Psychoanalysis, pp. 19–28.

Fairbairn, W.R.D. (1940). Schizoid Factors in the Personality. In *Psychoanalytic Studies of the Personality*, London: Routledge and Kegan Paul, 1952, pp. 3–27.

Kernberg, O. (1967). Borderline Personality Organization. *Journal of the American Psychoanalytic Association*, 15, pp. 641–685.

Little, M. (1958). On Delusional Transference (Transference Psychosis). *International Journal of Psychoanalysis*, 39, pp. 134–138.

Ogden, T. (1986). *The Matrix of the Mind*. Northvale, NJ and London: Jason Aronson.

Ogden, T. (1989). *The Primitive Edge of Experience*. Northvale, NJ and London: Jason Aronson.

Searles, H.F. (1963). Transference Psychosis in the Psychotherapy of Chronic Schizophrenia. *International Journal of Psycho-Analysis*, 44, pp. 249–281.

Winnicott, D.W. (1960). Ego Distortion in Terms of True and False Self. In *The Maturational Processes and the Facilitating Environment*. New York: International Universities Press, 1965, pp. 140–152.

Winnicott, D.W. (1967). The Use of the Object and Relating Through Cross-Identification. In *Playing and Reality*. New York: Basic Books, 1971, pp. 86–94.

7

"ATTACKS ON LINKING" AS ATTACKS ON THE FORMATION OF THE LYRICAL DIMENSION

In his paper "Attacks on Linking" (1959), Bion argues that it is through projective identification that the patient (or the infant) can investigate his or her own feelings in a personality (either the therapist's or the mother's) powerful enough to contain them. As said, the projection of bad or good contents onto the mother's psyche is a type of creation or modification of the mother by her infant in terms of his emergent self. A baby who projects persecutory feelings onto the mother in fact "creates" her in both his own experience as well as hers as a persecutor. A mother whose continuous self is overly rigid will not allow this to happen because, however momentary, the distortion will be insupportable to her. A mother whose continuous self, by contrast, is too weak or fragile, will be affected permanently, unable to "return" the infant's projections after processing them. Such a mother will become the concrete realization of her infant's projections. Sound development, in either one of these cases, will be impaired. The child of the first mother will hardly be able to evolve an active, potent emergent self; while the child of the second mother will form a domineering and destructive one. The child of the first mother will form a rigid and persecutory continuous self; while the child of the second mother will develop a continuous self that is feeble and blurred. Each of these types of internalization will have extensive implications for the further development of the self. These types of attack on linking are, hence, types of attack on the lyrical dimension.

Bion opens his paper with the following words:

> In previous papers I have had occasion, in talking of the psychotic part of the personality, to speak of the destructive attacks which the patient makes on anything which is felt to have the function of linking one object with another.
>
> *(Bion, 1959, p. 308)*

According to Bion, the attack on thinking processes actually destroys the ability to be conscious of external as well as internal reality. One efficient way of achieving this is by the annihilation of any linking that would lead to verbal thought. The link under attack is the one responsible for any fertile connection, whether between mother and baby, between analyst and patient, between the various parts of the self, or between a certain pre-conception and its realization. Once the link has been destroyed the two objects can no longer fruitfully connect. As a result, symbolization becomes impossible. Symbolization, as mentioned earlier, is the process whereby two objects join and reveal their similarity while also maintaining their separate identities. Where an attack on linking occurs the various objects become either indistinguishable, or alternatively can no longer be connected on a common basis.

As we have seen, the attack on the integration between the continuous and the emergent can take various forms and obeys to a variety of control mechanisms. But damage to the dialectics between emergent and continuous will always ensue in damage to the capacity for symbolization. This will be due to one of the following dysfunctions: dysfunction in synthetic ability (such as in the case of the schizoid personality) or dysfunction in analytic ability (such as in the case of the borderline personality). If the continuous self is internalized as rejecting the emergent self, the damage to the symbolizing function will be expressed in an impaired synthetic ability, since the similar and the different (the permanent and the changing, the general and the singular) are internalized as mutually exclusive and resisting any connection. If, on the other hand, the emergent is internalized as swallowing the continuous, the symbolic function will be affected in the form of an impaired analytic ability, because the general and the singular, the permanent and the changing are perceived as losing their distinct qualities within synthesis. Since the process of symbolization relies on the combination of analysis and synthesis – on the ability to grasp what is similar between two elements (through the continuous self) while at the same time preserving their singular, distinct qualities (by means of the emergent self) – a proper symbolic function will not be able to evolve in either one of these cases.

To return to "Attacks on Linking", Bion writes in note 95, entitled "Curiosity, Arrogance and Stupidity":

> In the paper I presented at the International Congress of 1957 I suggested that Freud's analogy of an archaeological investigation with a psycho-analysis would have been helpful if it were considered that we were exposing evidence not so much of a primitive civilization as of a primitive disaster. The value of the analogy is lessened because in the analysis we are confronted not so much with a static situation that permits leisurely study, but with a catastrophe that remains at one and the same moment actively vital and yet incapable of resolution into quiescence.
>
> *(Bion, 1959, p. 311)*

Elsewhere in the same note he writes:

> Attacks on the link originate in what Melanie Klein calls the paranoid-schizoid phase. This period is dominated by part-object relationships. If it is borne in mind that the patient has a part-object relationship with himself as well as with objects not himself, it contributes to the understanding of phrases such as "it seems" which are commonly employed by the deeply disturbed patient on occasions when a less disturbed patient might say "I think" or "I believe". When he says "it seems" he is often referring to a feeling – an "it seems" feeling – which is a part of his psyche and yet is not observed as part of a whole object. The conception of the part-object as analogous to an anatomical structure, encouraged by the patient's employment of concrete images as units of thought, is misleading because the part-object relationship is not with the anatomical structures only but with function, not with anatomy but with physiology, not with the breast but with feeding, poisoning, loving, hating. This contributes to the impression of a disaster that is dynamic and not static.
>
> *(Bion, 1959, pp. 311–312)*

Its dynamic nature is a central component of the psychic catastrophe, argues Bion. It is not just the "breast" as a static object that was internalized as damaged, but the function of the breast, that is, the nurturing function, too, was internalized as such. It was not the maternal object that has been internalized as impaired but the maternal object's function – the function of love – that was internalized as such. Bion suggests that psychopathology originates not in the internalization of impaired objects, or indeed part-objects, but in the acute damage to the internalization of the linking function between objects in its various aspects: love, hate, nurturing and poisoning. We could say, in terms of the interaction between the emergent and the continuous principles of the self, that psychopathology is not merely associated with the internalization of a domineering "emergent" principle or a persecutory "continuous" one, but with the psyche's profound attack on their integration; that is, on the function of the lyrical dimension. The outcome of the damage to this function does not only relate to the self's ability to be in touch with an external object, but also to its ability to link between internal objects, or in other words: its ability to allow for interaction between all the internal expressions of the emergent and the continuous. As a result of this impairment, all derivatives of three-dimensional thinking will be affected, along with the ability for curiosity and love.

According to Britton, in his article "Subjectivity, Objectivity and Triangular Space" (1998), it is the child's perception, in the course of his normal development, of his parents coming together – independently of him – that unifies his psychic world. The perception of his parents as one unit creates in the child's imagination one world in which various object relations can occur, rather than "monadic" serial worlds, each marked by its own particular object relationships. The primal family triangle provides the child with two types of link that connect him with each parent separately, and confront him also with the link between the parents, leaving him as an external observer.

Initially, the parental link is conceived in primitive part-object terms. If the link between the parents perceived in love and hate can be tolerated in the child's psyche, it provides the child with a prototype for an object relationship of a third kind, in which he features as a witness and not as a participant. This is how, within the infantile psyche, a "third position" evolves; a position from which the subject is able to observe object relationships. If this type of position actually comes into being, it enables us to also tolerate being observed. This is the basis for our ability to see ourselves as we are interacting with others and for entertaining another point of view while simultaneously maintaining our own. Britton argues that this third position affords us the complex capacity of "observing ourselves while being ourselves" (Briton, 1998, pp. 41–42). The psychological freedom thus gained, Britton calls the "triangular space". This is the space that emerges as a result of the child's ability to tolerate the link between the primary maternal object – representing the subjective sensitive self – and the third object, i.e. the father, who represents objective perceptions. The centre of Britton's article, which is dedicated to the psychological implications of impairment of the triangular space, is formed by the proposed distinction between two clinical states resulting in two personality structures. He calls the first of these conditions: "the thin-skinned syndrome" and the second: "thick-skinned narcissism: hyper objectivity":

> What I suggest is that these two clinical states, thin-skinnedness and thick-skinnedness, are the result of two different relationships of the *subjective self* with the *third object* within the internal Oedipus situation.
>
> *(Briton, 1998, p. 46)*

According to Britton, the third object is experienced as foreign to the sensitive subjective self. In the thin-skinned syndrome, the self tries to avoid the objectivity of the third object and clings to subjectivity. In the thick-skinned syndrome, by contrast, the self identifies with the third object, and adopts the latter's characteristic objectivity while rejecting his own subjectivity. While some people, Britton argues, live either in one state or in the other, others alternate between them. When the thin-skinned syndrome dominates, the person is described as borderline. When the thick-skinned syndrome takes the upper hand, the person is described as schizoid. The patient in the hyper-subjective condition (thin-skinned syndrome) wants to swallow the therapist into his subjective world. For this to occur, any difference between the patient's version of the therapist and the latter's own personality must be erased.[1] In the hyper-objective condition, by contrast, the therapeutic alliance relies on a denial of the subjective experience of the patient–therapist relationship.[2]

Describing the borderline dynamic, Britton argues that its centre-stage is taken by a destructive duel between the subjective and the objective reality, and between the private and the general. Characterizing the transference patterns of the hyper-subjective (borderline) patient, Britton argues that in terms of the Oedipal triangle, so long as the therapist goes along with, and encourages, the personal, emergent thoughts of the patient, he will be experienced as the understanding maternal object. As soon, however, as he offers his own thoughts, whether based on general experience or on psychoanalytical theories, he is felt like the father who interferes with the patient's most personal and internal self, pushing the latter out of his subjective context into the objective sphere.[3] This is an Oedipal situation with a defensive structure, which includes a fantasy of a maternal object with total empathy and passive understanding, and of an aggressive paternal figure who forcibly imposes objectivity. Such a structure guarantees that the psyche will never experience a re-integration between the understanding object and the not-understanding object (that is, between representations of the mother and the father) since such integration would lead to the final and absolute annihilation of understanding.

The two clinical states described here (the thin- and thick-skinned syndromes) result in two distinct modes of transference: while the hyper-subjective (thin-skinned) patient will mainly ask for empathic acceptance, the hyper-objective (thick-skinned) patient will want responses based on objective knowledge, which is the only type of knowledge he accepts as meaningful. Both states, however, share their greatest fear, which is the fear from linking between the embracing, encompassing transference and the penetrating transference, namely the possible linking between subjectivity and objectivity. Thus, the anxieties of hyper-subjective and hyper-objective patients have something in common: in both cases, anxiety concerns a psychic state that resembles mythic and literary descriptions of primordial chaos, with its characteristics of confusion and boundlessness. What distinguishes between the two states is a difference of emphasis: while hyper-objective patients mainly fear the emptiness, darkness and bottomlessness of chaos – that is, the complete absence of boundaries – the hyper-subjective patients fear the destruction of meaning and the incomprehensibility of chaos (Britton, 1998, p. 53). The basic human wish for "a well-defined world in which it is possible to find meaning" (Britton, 1998), which I mentioned at the outset of this book as representative of the wish for an integration between the emergent and the continuous principles of the self, hence unites both the primordial wishes and the primordial anxieties of both types of personality mentioned above.

Bion (1959) clarified that the infant does not experience the mother's inability to take in his projections as a simple failure, but rather as a destructive and intended attack by her on his link and communication with her as his good object. Britton argued that in this kind of situation the only way to retain the mother as a good object in the child's mind is by denying the experience of her impermeability and by attributing the disturbance in understanding to another (third) object (who is neither the mother nor the child). This process generates a fantasy of a hostile third force with destructive powers, putting the communicational link between mother and child under permanent threat of destruction. In the Oedipal situation, this hostile force is equated with the father. Whenever the child imagines or witnesses a link between the two parents he experiences the threat of the mother's being reconstituted as a non-receptive, malignantly misunderstanding maternal object. Thus, whenever the child has a mental image of his parents together in a kind of primal scene, it will be experienced as initiating a mental catastrophe.

What, however, is the nature of this catastrophe? For Britton, the deepest fear is of what he calls "malignant misunderstanding". By this he means an experience of being so misunderstood, in such a fundamental and powerful way, that one's experience of oneself would be eliminated and thus the possibility of the self establishing meaning would be annihilated. It is the fear of a return to primordial chaos, something that corresponds to Bion's (1962) "nameless dread". Here what *has not been understood* (due to the mother's failure) transforms into something that *cannot be understood*. All ancient religions, Britton argues, recognize one power that is in charge of understanding, order and meaning, which is threatened by a dark counter-force that rules over primeval chaos.

Freud (1933) located the primordial chaos in the id and wrote of *fear of the id* as fundamental. Bion's notion of *nameless dread* refers to the fear of being overwhelmed by uncontained, untransformed, psychic elements. When the child experiences the mother's misunderstanding as an attack rather than as a failure, what evolves is a psychic experience of a destructive force, a force that is aimed to prevent any possibility of self-knowledge and of finding meaning. If, according to Britton, this propensity for malignant misunderstanding returns to the primary maternal object, the latter becomes the prototype of an object of desire, which is at the same time a menace to individual integrity and self-coherence. This, then, causes love to arouse unbearable existential anxiety.

In the case of the borderline personality (thin-skinned syndrome), the primary object is preserved, by means of splitting, as devoted to empathic understanding (i.e. to subjective perception), as a result of which love remains possible, on the condition that it remains free of objective appraisal. This creates in fantasy a third object as the source of malignant misunderstanding and as a constant threat to the empathic mutual understanding between self and primary object. When, at certain points, the splitting collapses and the person experiences himself simultaneously as subject and object – this is accompanied by a sense of disaster. The mother and the father – united in the analyst's gaze – become a monstrous combined object, due to the integration it encapsulates.

There is, doubtlessly, a significant connection between the notion of the triangular space that ensues from the integration between the objective and the subjective perceptions, and the formation of the lyrical dimension as a result of the integration between the emergent (which includes subjective perceptions) and the continuous (which includes the objective perception of the self and of the world). What, then, are the differences between them? While the emergent principle of the self includes subjective perception – it is not identical to it. What we are dealing with is a broader aspect of self experiences; one that embraces the grasp of the world not only from within but also in terms of constant change. Correspondingly we can say that while the continuous principle of the self includes the objective perception of the world it still does not coincide with it, as its essence is not just objectivity but also the constant, the common, the predictable and the explicable. In fact we can formulate the emergent self as the necessary ground for subjective perception, while the continuous self supplies the necessary ground for objective perceptions.

Would it be right to consider the emergent as the representation of the primary (maternal) object, while taking the continuous as the representation of the "third", the "other", the father? Only in a very limited sense. I tend to regard the emergent and the continuous as the internalizations of the emergent and the continuous principles related to both the mother and the father, as well as to their patterns of interaction between themselves as well as with their child.[4] What I mean is that in any interaction, with whatever object, there feature an emergent principle, a continuous principle and an emergent/continuous interaction, which is internalized as a pattern. Wherever a possibility for fertile interaction between these two principles occurs, integration is internalized. This will be the case whether the emergent is situated in the other and the continuous in the self, or it is a matter of internalizing the entire interaction between emergent and continuous as they appear in the other.

Each time such an integration is internalized – and it should be stressed again that this is a dynamic, unending process, not a developmental "stage" – the self gains another dimension of depth: a lyrical dimension. The lyrical dimension forms not merely the basis of our ability to know ourselves and to be ourselves simultaneously, or of our ability to preserve, at one and the same time, our own perspective and that of the other, but it is what allows us to have an experience of truthfulness, multi-dimensionality and eternity. This is the dimension that gives the psyche its ability to believe and to dream. This is the dimension that carries hope and motion, the ability to accept the limits of reality while maintaining the infinite desire for change.

What I have said so far is compatible with many aspects of Britton's description of the triangular dynamic that produces the hyper-subjective (borderline) structure and the hyper-objective (schizoid) structure. The borderline patient's close adherence to the subjective experience of the world, and his or her experience of the objective point of view as destructive of self as well as of the capacity for relationship and love, is indeed familiar to analysts and therapists from their daily encounters with borderline patients. But experiencing the objective as destructive and opposing love is only one side of the borderline dynamic. The other side involves the experience of the singular, the emergent, as invading the continuous, the objective, effacing its outlines and changing it beyond recognition. The borderline person's love cannot include an "objective" side, not only because it is felt as obliterating this love, but also because love itself is perceived, too, as obliterating the objective side and as annihilating its boundaries. In the borderline person's love, the emergent aspect comes to dominate the continuous one to such an extent that it would seem as though the continuous aspect had never arisen in

the self in the first place, and as though there is absolutely no possibility of being in any form of dialogue with the continuous aspect of the world.

Britton's description of the schizoid structure is more amenable to what I have been saying earlier in this context. The total adoption of the objective viewpoint runs parallel, at least to some extent, to the way in which, in my earlier description, a persecutory, rigid continuous principle takes the upper hand over the emergent. My claim, however, is that even though the mother's difficulty in containing the infant's projections is experienced by the latter as an active attack, this is not an attack on the link between the infant and the mother, but one on the link between the continuous – which at this point in time is experienced as the mother's outline – and the infantile emergent which is trying to re-create it through its projections.

A mother who does not allow for her infant's projections, that is, does not allow her infant to "create" her in terms of his emergent self, acts in this way because her continuous self is persecutory, fragile and lacks the flexibility needed in order to contain the new projection without this annihilating its boundaries. Such a mother, however, will reveal the same kind of interaction between her own continuous and emergent principles, and this interaction pattern, too, will be internalized by her infant. Eventually, this mother will find it extremely hard to perceive her infant through "emergent" eyes. She will have difficulty letting herself experience her baby beyond what his objective features allow her. Her gaze on this baby will remain subjected to the rules of the continuous self and hence, in her eyes, he will forever remain "clever", or "handsome" or "nice", as fits his actual features, but will never gain that "princely aura" which the lyrical dimension bestows on its loved ones by releasing their "possible self" from their actual one. This pattern will be internalized and subsequently reflected in this child's difficulty in perceiving or experiencing himself in terms of his possible self, and hence also difficulty in loving and being loved, believing and being believed in, dreaming and being dreamt.

While the continuous self, through the experience of continuity, provides us with an axis, it is the emergent self that allows us to move along this axis. The integration between them is the "desire in itself" as it is struggling to exist within the confines and constraints of reality. And so the lyrical dimension is not just in charge of the integration between the singular and the general, but also of the link between movement and direction and between the desire and the object at which this desire directs itself. When this dimension is impaired, *desire turns objectless* and is left empty and indistinct (a state that characterizes the borderline structure), or alternatively *the object is being evacuated of desire* and is left sterile and flat (a state that is characteristic of the schizoid structure). The lyrical dimension, hence, is in charge not just of the three-dimensionality of the self, the object and the relationship between them, but also of all forms of internal linking between the desire and the object-of-desire: the link between the thought and the thinker, between the dream and the dreamer, and between every pre-conception and its actualization.

Notes

1 This dynamics very much resembles my earlier description of borderline dynamics in terms of the interaction between continuous and emergent, where it is assumed that in the borderline personality the emergent principle swallows the continuous principle.

2 Here too, there is a similarity between Britton's description and my earlier explanation concerning the schizoid dynamic, whereby a rigid persecutory continuous strangles all manifestations of the emergent self.

3 This experience, as I understand it, resembles – in some sense – what happens when the Winnicottian mother forces the baby to take in a premature recognition of separation.

4 Can we nevertheless say that the emergent is a female principle while the continuous is masculine, and that each is found in different measures in the father and the mother respectively? I am not sure either. We could equally regard the emergent principle – which actively and willfully creates the world – as a masculine principle, while regarding the continuous principle – which receives the world as it is – as a feminine one.

References

Bion, W.R. (1959). Attacks on Linking. *International Journal of Psychoanalysis*, 40, pp. 308–315.

Bion, W.R. (1962). The Psycho-Analytic Study of Thinking. *International Journal of Psycho-Analysis*, 43, pp. 306–310.

Britton, R. (1998). Subjectivity, Objectivity and Triangular Space. In *Belief and Imagination*. London: Routledge, in association with the Institute of Psychoanalysis, pp. 41–58.

Freud, S. (1933). New Introductory Lectures on Psycho-analysis. S.E., 22. London: Hogarth Press, pp. 1–182.

8

THE LINE THAT DIVIDES SLEEPING FROM WAKING

The malignant interaction between the emergent principle and the continuous principle in *My Michael* by Amos Oz

On the basis of my argument so far, I would like now to offer a reading of Amos Oz's book *My Michael* in terms of the interaction between inside and outside in Hannah Gonen, the novel's protagonist. This interaction can be seen as a kind of "malignant containment" relation between her emergent self and continuous self.

In fact, Hannah Gonen's psychic repertoire reveals two types of malignant containment. The first of these is one in which the container (the continuous self) suffocates the contained (the emergent self). In the second, the contained stretches the container until the latter reaches its breaking point. Not only do these two types of containment occur in Hannah Gonen's intrapsychic world – between, that is, the different dimensions of her own psyche – but they also obtain in her relations with Michael. In this relationship, Michael represents the continuous element, which is responsible for the reality principle and for the notion of the world as steady and intelligible, while Hannah has the monopoly over the emergent element, which experiences the world as in endless flux and pulls the personal, idiosyncratic perception of it to its pathological extreme.

In this context, the malignant interaction between Hannah and Michael is the same malignant interaction that is taking place within Hannah's own psychic world. The pattern repeats itself with horrifying precision: wherever the continuous is allowed to exist, it strangles the emergent. Wherever the emergent is given the right to express itself, it silences the continuous. Since integration between these two dimensions of the self is impossible, Hannah Gonen is increasingly forced to make the tragic choice between the two sides of this split.

A first manifestation in the novel's narrative of the hiatus between the internal world (representing the emergent self) and the outside world (representing the continuous self) is the relative importance of the realm of dreams compared to that of reality. Unlike in most literary texts, where dreams often have a kind of illustrative function, bearing out psychological structures that feature in the narrative, in the case of Hannah Gonen, her dreams do not offer windows overlooking into her psyche, but constitute the only space in which any psychic life is possible at all. This is not just a case of a doubling between the "real" and the phantasmatic world, but also one of deep and malignant antagonism between them. And so, in a unique parallel process, the structure of the book becomes identical to that of Hannah Gonen's psyche, while the internal and the external objects face each other with varying degrees of hostility or affinity: Michael Gonen, the grey, reserved, submissive, dry-witted man contrasts with Michael Strogoff, the invincible hero of the inner world whose eyes are filled with blue metal. And Hannah Gonen herself, the quiet, introverted student is set against her dream-double: a princess who holds the strangers that humiliate her tight in her sadomasochistic grip – "Yvonne Azoulay" who is awaiting her heroic liberation at the hand of Captain Nemo.

Arab twins make appearances throughout the novel, at times featuring as dream figures, at others as a recollection. Their role in Hannah's psychic world is complex and symbolic. As befits a twin, their status is two-fold: they are in fact the novel's only characters who belong neither to an inside nor to an outside, but rather exist simultaneously in both. Halil and Aziz are actual figures from Hannah Gonen's childhood: they were the sons of an Arab sheikh who lived near her home. When she was a young girl she used to play games with them in which she dominated the two, at times, while at other times she was humiliated by them. Since they did not share the same language, they played without words using what she calls "guttural sounds" (p. 21). The hallucinatory nature of the play is apparently what caused it to become a main theme in her adult fantasies and dreams. But the twins represent not only her passionate unconscious but also the very split that runs both across her psyche and through the plot: it is the split between inside and outside, between true and fantastic, between mental and physical.

"I felt that this wasn't, by no manner of means, the first time" – Hannah keeps saying in this context over and over again, as she looks on at what is happening in her small world with a sense that everything has already happened before. This is not an ordinary *déjà vu* experience. The illusion originates in the real doubleness that characterizes her life as she simultaneously manages two orders of time, two worlds. This complexity multiplies when doubleness proves also to yield inversion: it is the inner world that is felt as the true world while the outside world is a kind of cover. Life actually resembles a dream-work, where the overt story is the one that unfolds in reality, while the hidden story, the true one, is being told in parallel. Inside, colorful, strong and wild characters spring into existence and lively narratives unfold, while daily reality is death: a grey, banal routine through which the characters plod, sinking ever deeper into their isolation, loneliness and depression.

The gap between inside and outside is also reflected in the form of dialogue. While the external characters exchange only brief, stunted and laconic sentences, whenever Hannah dives into her inner world her sentences grow longer and richer. Still, in spite of Hannah's inner flourishing of words, communication between her inner characters is "symbiotic", even semiotic in nature, one in which they understand each other by the merest gesture, from the way the body tends. Here, too, inversion occurs: in her real life, Hannah Gonen is considered "a woman of words": she studies literature; the neighbours' son tries to consult her about his poems; even though she does not write poems herself, Michael's father believes she is a poet. Her words, however, do not bridge the abyss but rather turn, in a tragic inversion, into what actually creates the abyss between her and the other. Hannah Gonen's use of words is elusive: one that creates rather than reduces distance; one that covers up rather than reveals; one that blurs rather than clarifies. When Yair, her son, approaches her with his questions she either replies with misleading answers or silences him. When Michael attempts to understand her, she leads him astray intentionally. Communication, for her, is a humiliating effort, a struggle doomed to end with her surrender to a sense that she will never be truly understood.

Along with the wish to be understood without words, Hannah Gonen also has a part that refuses to be revealed. This part wants to guard the isolated, non-communicative core whose disclosure might prove too destructive for the vulnerable self. In the case of Hannah Gonen, however, this inner core is taking over. It grows more voluminous at the expense of the realistic discourse, which wears increasingly thinner.

"In the literature of the Hebrew enlightenment there are frequent references to the conflict between light and darkness", she writes. "The writer is committed to the eventual triumph of light. I must say that I prefer the darkness" (p. 16).

Under the cover of darkness occurs the inner fermentation of all those geological elements that Michael, in reality, "dries" in his dull doctoral study on processes of erosion in the gorges of the Faran desert. This is a matchlessly evocative image of what happens in the tragic transition between inside and outside: on their way to yielding the learned doctorate, the picturesque erosive processes transform into an inventory of lifeless data. Observing Michael as he talks about his dissertation, Hannah says:

> The relaxed pose of his body in the armchair as he talks about volcanic eruptions, about the cooling of the crystalline crust. Those words come out of the dreams which I dream, and into those dreams they shall return.
>
> *(Oz, 1972, p. 134)*

Not only is she aware of the "death" of these materials as they make their way out from the inside; she regards the source of all materials as being located inside. Thus, not only is the dream the source of everything – but everything will revert into dream as well. Again, we witness an inversion: rather than that the source of the dream is in reality, the source of reality is what occurs in dreams.

On the birth of her son, Yair, Hannah is assailed by dread. The child, who concretely symbolizes the possible transition from inside to outside arouses her fear and rejection, because there is something in him of both inside and outside, at one and the same time:

> Between periods of sleep the baby would open his eyelids and display islands of pure blue. I felt that this was his inner color, that the peepholes of his eyes revealed mere droplets of the radiant blue which filled the baby's body underneath his skin. When my son looked at me I remembered that he could not see yet. The thought frightened me. I did not trust nature to repeat successfully the established sequence of events.
>
> *(Oz, 1972, p. 65)*

In fact, the fear that the baby will remain full of the blue, inner material and fail to see is two-fold: the fear, on the one hand, is that the transition from inside to outside will never be accomplished and the baby will stay blind to the external world. And on the other hand, there is a fear that this shift will actually take place, making the child lose the internal "radiant blue", thus becoming "inwardly" blind. At a later stage, indeed, she writes: "The islands of pure blue turned into small, inquisitive grey eyes" (p. 67).

One of her dreams reveals a crack that "quickly widened and spread like a railway-network in an instructional film, where processes are shown speeded up" (p. 61). The crack between inside and outside grows steadily wider; the tension between them increases, becomes more desperate, with the former taking over the latter. Gradually, the dreams become hallucinations, and no longer is it only at night that the inside invades the outside: it also happens during the wakeful hours of the day. We may say that instead of the emergent self developing safely within the boundaries of the continuous self, here, the emergent stretches the boundaries of the continuous until bursting. This invasion of the emergent into the continuous, or this usurpation of the outside by the inside reaches a climax when Hannah awakes one day before dawn with a very sore throat. Acting on a destructive addiction she takes off her clothes and takes a cold shower, reaches a kind of orgasm of pain and desire, allows hallucinations to take over reality, her body, her voice, and resuscitates a vague, old longing "to fall seriously ill", sick unto death:

> I have fond memories of an attack of diphtheria I suffered as a child of nine. [. . .] According to the doctor, Dr. Rosenthal, there are some children who prefer to be ill, who refuse to be cured, because illness offers, in a sense, a state of freedom. When I recovered, [. . .] I had lost my powers of alchemy, the ability to make my dreams carry me over the line that divides sleeping from waking. To this day I feel a sense of disappointment on waking. I mock at my vague longing to fall seriously ill.
>
> *(Oz, 1972, p. 15)*

Here too, we observe the same tragic inversion: it is not the sickness that takes hold of her, but Hannah who holds on to the sickness. The dreams do not draw her into themselves, but Hannah herself pulls them beyond the line that divides sleeping from waking. Illness is not where the crash occurs: it happens when she recovers, that is to say, in the transition back from inside to outside which always involves capitulation to the reality principle. Illness, it becomes clear, is where she can finally feel that she exists: "I had a body and it was mine" she writes, "and it throbbed and thrilled and was alive" (p. 148). Reality, thus, expropriates her from herself, while psychosis – or illness – are her way of regaining ownership of her body and psyche. Illness constitutes a "state of freedom" because it allows the emergent self to take command over the psyche's front. The creative, the singular and the private prevail over the perception of reality and subdue its principles.

As time passes, it becomes more and more of an effort to stay in touch with the outside world. Hannah adopts all kinds of clichés in an attempt to sound relevant, but, as the inside progressively stifles the outside, she's hallucinating most of the day. In one touching moment she goes out into the street for the first time after recovering from her severe illness, and realizes that a noise that was going on inside her has actually stopped:

> For the first time since Michael's departure I got up and went outside. It made a change. As if some shrill, piercing sound had suddenly stopped. As if a motor which had been trilling outside all day had suddenly been switched off towards evening. The sound had passed unnoticed all day; only when it stopped did it make itself felt. A sudden stillness. It had existed and now it had stopped. It had stopped, therefore it had existed.
>
> *(Oz, 1972, p. 172)*

In fact it was the sound of her interior – the constantly noisy interior that separates her from the outside; the emergent element locked in a perennial struggle for her heart against reality and its rules, much like the hallucinated twins, Halil and Aziz, who act as though their movements were in harmony but were actually engaged in a titanic fight trying to win her love.

A dialogue between her and Michael about the difference between the trite and the true goes on throughout the book, right from its start:

> Michael said: "everybody has strong and weak points. You would probably call that a trite remark. You'd be right. But trite isn't the opposite of true. Two twos are four is a trite remark, but nevertheless . . ."
>
> "Nevertheless, Michael, trite *is* the opposite of true and one day I shall go mad like Doba Glick and it'll be your fault, Doctor goofy Ganz".
>
> *(Oz, 1972, p. 196)*

This, it could be said, is the essence of her suffering. Though it doesn't clash with the correct, the trite is the opposite of true. And it is so not because it is not based firmly in logic, but because the trite is the reality principle's secret weapon in its bid to usurp spaces from the inner reality, territories that will not be restored to the latter's authority. This is the essence of the struggle between inside and outside: if the great weapon of the inside is its creativity, the most fatal weapon of the outside is the trite.

And indeed, as the book draws to an end, the heroes of the internal and the external take their positions for a last duel: Michael Gonen, the hero of reality and trite versus Michael Strogoff, the mythic hero of the internal truth. The one person's war versus that of the other; the one person's defeat versus the other's victory. In the wake of this the crushing triumph of the internal reality over the external reality is proclaimed. While Michael Gonen concedes defeat without fighting, Michael Strogoff prevails by the grace of power and love:

> One day, as I was coming from the clinic where I used to go for a lengthy treatment for my throat and vocal chords, Michael came out of the house and advanced towards me. [. . .] There was bad news on his face. He had suffered a minor disaster, he said. "Disaster, Michael?" "A minor disaster". Apparently he had just seen the latest number of the official journal of the Royal Geological Society of Great Britain, which contained an article by a well-known professor from Cambridge, propounding a new and rather startling theory about erosion. Certain assumptions which were fundamental to Michael's thesis had been brilliantly disproved. "That's marvelous," I said. "Now's your chance, Michael Gonen. You show this Englishman what's what. Pulverise him. Don't give in." "I can't," Michael said sheepishly. "It's out of the question. He's right. I'm convinced."
>
> *(Oz, 1972, p. 200)*

And further on:

> I thought to myself: When Strogoff was captured by the cruel Tartars they planned to put out his eyes with red-hot irons. Strogoff was a hard man, but he also had a lot of love. Because of his love his eyes filled with tears. These tears of love saved him, because they cooled the red-hot irons. Will-power and cunning enabled him to pose as a blind man until he had completed the difficult mission entrusted to him by the Czar in St. Petersburg. The mission and the agent alike were saved by love and strength.
>
> *(Oz, 1972, p. 201)*

Michael Gonen's defeat, in a sense, symbolizes the defeat of the realistic component as such; the triumph of the internal world over the external. From that moment on, when the subjects of the internal world, freed from their captivity, move out to take control of all the territories of physical as well as mental existence, the undisputed rule of the inside over the outside, of the emergent over the continuous, is installed:

> But I have more left than mere words. I am still able to unfasten a heavy padlock. To part the iron gates. To set free two twin brothers, who will slip out into the vast night to do my bidding. I shall urge them on.
>
> *(Oz, 1972, p. 214–215)*

This release does not constitute a resolution of the split by means of integration. On the contrary: the result is such further deepening of the rift between the split-off parts that they become entirely severed from each other. For Hannah Gonen, who has one foot planted on each opposing side of the ever-widening abyss, the one way of not collapsing into that abyss is by giving up on one of the sides and staying put, with all her might, on the other. Her choice can be seen as suicidal. But it can equally be viewed as a last-ditch effort to maintain a sense of vitality and freedom. At the heart of the titanic struggle between inside and outside, between the emergent and the continuous, and between psychic death and madness, she tragically opts for madness, since for her this equals the choice for life; for inside madness "her power to love" is maintained, even if it is only in the confines of her own psyche.

Reference

Oz, A. (1972). *My Michael*, trans. Nicholas de Lange. London: Chatto & Windus.

9

MELANCHOLIA AS MOURNING
OVER A POSSIBLE OBJECT[1]

The experience of loss is undoubtedly one of the most fundamental experiences of mental existence. The way in which this experience takes place, with its infinite number of variations, carries within itself not only the psychic code of coping with situations of loss, but also the psychic code of coping with the course of life as such.

It may be said that the experience of loss, any loss, has two main dimensions. The first is the *actual* dimension of loss. This dimension is responsible for the touchstone of reality, and therefore echoes the absence of the lost object from the objective world. The second is the *possible* dimension of loss.[2] This dimension is responsible for the continuation of the internalized dialogue of the mourner with the object of mourning, despite of and in addition to its objective absence. It is this dimension that is in charge of the capacity to identify in the absent object those aspects which do not disappear once it is gone: those aspects which were present as a possibility rather than as an actualization, and therefore may not be annihilated with its actual existence.

The relationships between these two dimensions of experience, or between these two aspects of the self, are varied. When the actual is overly dominant in relation to the possible, it may be assumed that the subject will cling to the non-existence of the beloved object, putting itself to death together with it. When the possible predominates the actual, on the other hand, the subject may cling to the psychotic illusion that the lost object still exists. The preservation of this illusion will, of course, involve a lower degree of reality testing. These are, in fact, two types of pathological mourning, though the second type would have manic characteristics, perhaps as an inversion of the melancholic core.

This chapter is dedicated, however, not only to the discussion of normal verses pathological mourning, but also to the discussion of the distinction between pathological mourning and melancholia. In this context, I intend to show that whereas pathological mourning, however extreme it might be, is mourning over an *actual object* – melancholia constitutes mourning over a *possible* one.

In a state of melancholia an individual does not mourn over an actual object, such as a job one has lost, or a person who has rejected one's love, but over the loss of a possible object, that is to say, over one's being incapable of working and of being loved. In other words, although the melancholic looks like he or she is mourning over an actual object – in fact s/he does not distinguish it from the possible one; when the dividing line between the actual and the possible is eradicated, mourning acquires the quality of totality, thus becomes melancholia.

As mentioned earlier, the experience of selfhood is constituted through the integration of all the momentary experiences of the self. The sense that "one is incomprehensible" is not tantamount to the sum of moments during which one has felt "not understood". Rather, it is a generalization that exceeds the sum of these moments and becomes a kind of formative experience: an experiential mould into which one will pour, from now on, every new experience and by means of which one will render such experiences meaningful. Thus, the experience of selfhood is not an aggregation of individual assumptions ("Y doesn't understand me", or "X loves me") but the integration of these assumptions into a generalized experience: "I am incomprehensible", or, alternatively: "I am lovable". Between these two types of experience, that of being "misunderstood" or "loved" applies to the *actual self*, whereas "incomprehensible" or "lovable" applies to the *possible self*. It is, in fact, an experience that has undergone a transformation from the actual to the possible: it has been generalized and assimilated into the self as a constitutive experience of a possibility or impossibility.

When the actual has ceased to exist (for instance, in the case of death), the work of mourning is based on the supposition that the possible continues to exist. In the mind of a mother who lost her child, the child can continue to grow as a possibility, indeed as an infinite number of possibilities, although his growth is continuously shrouded by the knowledge of his absence.[3] Similarly, the mother's *possible motherhood* can continue, even though her *actual motherhood* was cut short. She can console herself by writing to her dead child, by continuing her internal dialogue with him, even by posthumous reconciliation with him. On the other hand, if her motherhood is dependent on the actual rather than the possible aspect, when she loses her actual child she also loses her identity as a mother. Such a mother will find it hard to overcome her actual loss, since she won't be able to make the mental return-journey from the actual to the possible.

A patient whose young child recently died told me about a dream she dreamt. In that dream she was walking round children's shoe shops, choked with tears. She knew that her son was dead, but even so, she was looking for shoes for him, trying to work out his shoe size had he still been alive. She went into a shop and chose winter shoes, knowing that she would buy him new shoes every year, since within herself he would go on growing, and he would go on walking.

I reflected upon the words she chose and their ambiguity: he is growing within her, and the more he grows the more he walks (away from her), since, concomitantly with his growth, the knowledge of his being gone grows within her as well.

Death, and thereby the process of mourning, is to a great degree a process of return from the actual to the possible, just as birth is a transition from the possible to the actual. This may explain, for instance, the pathological mourner's attachment to mourning ceremonies as if they were actual or concrete objects. In fact, the concrete ceremonies of mourning may replace, as a kind of fetishistic object, the lost actual one, preventing the psyche from maintaining a living dialogue with the possible dimension of this object.

Let us consider another variation of mourning: that of the mourning process that the mother of a disabled child has to go through. Such a work of mourning depends in a way on the mother's integration of the *actual child* and the *possible child* that is locked within these actual limitations. Similarly, her working through her loss deeply depends on her ability to recognize the limitations of her *actual motherhood*, as well as being in touch with the *possible motherhood* locked within the actual one. In many cases, though, motherhood is revealed in its most beauty and greatness precisely in front of actual restrictions. Whenever this happens, it is a triumph of the possible over the actual.

What is the difference between a *possible* object and an *internal* one?

An internal object is always a reflection of an actual object, although it has gained, through the process of internalization, an independent status within the psychic space. It is, in fact, a type of memory, and this may be its main distinction in relation to the possible object. For whereas memory results from actual experience, the possible precedes this experience. The possible is not an entity that was ever actualized, then annihilated and now lives in memory or in the internal world, but one that was never actualized. Nonetheless – and here is where the essence of the link between them lies – the ability to internalize a lost object is connected to the ability to be in touch with its possible dimension.

The very act of internalization, as previously said, is a sort of transformation of the actual to the possible; therefore, internalization itself constitutes a work of mourning, which involves readiness to disengage from and take leave of the actual. In fact, the ability to internalize is deeply connected with the ability to identify the possible dimension of the object and to restore the object from its actual to its possible condition. A person that without a sufficiently developed sense of reality clings to the possible dimension of the object at the expense of the actual one, will not be able to complete processes of internalization, for internalization must begin with the actual. Such a person will replace internalization by projection: he or she will project his or her own possible dimension on the actual dimension of the other instead of extricating the possible dimension of the other from the (other's) actual one. But neither will a person who clings to the actual traits of the object be able to complete its internalization. Attachment to the concrete, or the inability to disengage oneself from the actual, will also prevent one from extricating the possible from the object's actual existence.

Difficulty in internalizing will, then, prevent both of these types of personality from working through mourning. In the first instance (psychotic clinging to the possible object), the person will continue to carry on an apparently "actual" dialogue with the lost object, refusing to recognize that it no longer exists and continuing to revive it psychotically in a manner increasingly remote from the actual. In the other case, the person will cling obsessively to mourning ceremonies and refuse to refrain from them, since their actual existence replaces and ensures the continued existence of the actual object relations, and their cessation might confront him with their definite loss.

It is important to remember that both reviving the object and clinging to mourning ceremonies exist in every process of working through loss. But even if they are not considered pathological in themselves – their extreme expressions may turn from expressions of working through into something that replace mourning or separates between the mourner and mourning. Pathological mourning, thus, is a situation in which the process of mourning separates the mourner from the lost object as well as from his or her own grief.

In *Mourning and Melancholia*, Freud writes:

> The distinguishing mental features of melancholia are a profoundly painful dejection, cessation of interest in the outside world, loss of capacity to love, inhibition of all activity, and a lowering of the self regarding feelings to a degree that finds utterance in self-reproaches and self-revilings, and culminates in a delusional expectation of punishment.
>
> *(Freud, 1917, p. 252)*

Freud maintains that mourning displays similar characteristics, with the exception of one: it does not involve the impairment of self-image so characteristic of melancholia, even though it, too, is characterized by the diminution and curbing of the ego as a result of devotion to mourning.

Freud goes on to say:

> In what, now, does the work which mourning performs consist? I do not think there is anything far-fetched in presenting it in the following way: Reality testing has shown that the loved object no longer exists, and it proceeds to demand that all libido shall be withdrawn from its attachments to that object. This demand arouses understandable opposition – it is a matter of general observation that people never willingly abandon a libidinal position, not even, indeed, when a substitute is already beckoning to them. This opposition can be so intense that a turning away from reality takes place and a clinging to the object through the medium of a hallucinatory wishful psychosis. Normally, respect for reality gains the day. Nevertheless its orders cannot be obeyed at once.
>
> *(Freud, 1917, p. 244)*

In other words, the recognition that the beloved object has indeed ceased to exist in reality necessitates adaptation of the ego; and this adaptation involves gradual separation of the libido from all memories and expectations connected to that object. However, after the completion of the work of mourning, the ego is again free and uninhibited. In melancholia, on the other hand, the loss is not necessarily an actual loss. It may be what Freud calls "a conceptual loss": for instance, the loss of the object as an object of love rather than as an actual object. Freud maintains that the patient himself is not always conscious of this loss. Frequently he knows *whom* he has lost, but not *what* he has lost in relation to him. Thus, it is reasonable to relate melancholia in some way to an unconscious loss of an object, as distinct from mourning in which the loss is not at all unconscious.

I would now like to employ some of the hypotheses presented above in order to cast light on a particular aspect of the difference between melancholia and mourning. In the case of "the abandoned bride", for instance, which Freud adduces as an example of the loss of the object as an object of love rather than as an actual object, melancholia can be related not to the fact that the loss is "closed off from consciousness", but to what I called earlier *the transformation from the "unloved" to the "unlovable"*. The abandoned bride has to cope not only with the actual loss of her love-object, but also with the loss of a *possible object*: she does not only cope with the loss of the actual or imaginary possibility that she could ever rehabilitate the object as an object of love, but also with the loss of the imagined possibility that she herself will one day again be worthy and the recipient of love. This explains, for instance, the attenuation of the self-image that characterizes melancholia as opposed to mourning. Mourning is a state of injury to the actual. Melancholia is a state of injury to the possible. Therefore melancholic loss is broader than the state of mourning, and has implications both for the future and for the past. In other words, coping with the loss of a possible object demands coping not only with the loss of the future (which is characteristic of the state of mourning) but also with the loss of the past, since the loss of the possible paints the whole past in colours different from those that formerly characterized it.

> In mourning it is the world which has become poor and empty; in melancholia it is the ego itself.
>
> *(Freud, 1917, p. 254).*

Since in mourning, one is confronted with an actual loss, it is the actual world, outside the self that is emptied of the object of loss. And since in melancholia the loss is of a possible object, it is the self, in which the possible lies, which shrinks and grows empty.

Therefore, in Freud's words:

> He is not of the opinion that a change has taken place in him, but extends his self-criticism back over the past; he declares that he was never any better.
>
> *(Freud, 1917, p. 246)*

The melancholic activates a transformation that changes the experience of loss from an experience of *there is not* to an experience of *there cannot be*. This generalization creates a vicious circle that eventually undermines the possibility of the creation of psychic space, since it uses the actual in order to deny the possible, thus establishing a *pseudo potential-space* within which integration and generalization become an apparatus devoted to the destruction of the self instead of its growth.

This process explains the self-impoverishment characteristic of melancholia as distinct from mourning: the repeated generalizations – *I am unlovable, I am incomprehensible* eventually become integrated into a constitutive meta-generalization that signifies – *I am not capable or worthy of living*.

Thus, there are three variations of impairment of the sound work of mourning. The first is expressed in the *psychotic clinging to the possible object*, with an absolute denial of its actual absence. The second is expressed in the *refusal to give up the actual object*, while denying any living dialogue with its possible aspects; this is expressed in ritual-obsessive clinging to the concrete ceremonies of mourning as a substitute for the lost actual object. The third variation, that of melancholia, may appear together with either of the two previous ones: in this variation, *the actual is enlisted to negate the possible*, by integrating the actual negative experiences in a way that turns them into infrastructural constitutive experiences, thus transferring them from the field of the actual to the field of the possible in a way that gradually disintegrate the foundations of the self. This sophisticated practice actually imitates the normal work of integration of the self (which generalizes momentary experiences as a means of development) and creates *a simulated potential space* within which integration becomes a mode of self-negation. The first two variations belong to the category of pathological mourning; the third belongs to the category of melancholia, which, as has been remarked above, can appear together with either of the other two variations and reinforce their pathological character.

Thomas Ogden, in a chapter dealing with the work of mourning in his *Conversations at the Frontier of Dreaming*, writes:

> Mourning is not simply a form of psychological work; it is a process centrally involving the experience of *making* something, creating something adequate to the experience of loss. What is "made", and the experience of making it – which together might be thought of as "the art of mourning" – represent the individual's effort to meet, to be equal to, to do justice to, the fullness and complexity of his or her relationship to what has been lost, and to the experience of loss itself.
>
> The creativity involved in the art of mourning need not be the highly developed creativity of the talented artist. The notion of creativity, as I conceive it here, applies equally to "ordinary creativity", that is, to the creativity of everyday life. What one "makes" in the process of mourning – whether it be a thought, a feeling, a gesture, a perception, a poem, a response to a poem, or a conversation – is far less important than the experience of making it.
>
> *(Ogden, 2001, pp. 117–118)*

He concludes this remarkable chapter with the following words:

> An elegy does not begin with grief; it is an effort to achieve grief in the experience of writing. An elegy, unlike a eulogy, must take in and be equal to (which is not to say identical to) the full complexity of the life that has been lost. The language of a poem that is an elegy must be enlivened by the loss or death of the person or the aspect of oneself who is no longer. In other words, an elegy must capture in itself not the voice that has been lost, but a voice brought to life in the experiencing of that loss – a voice enlivened by the experience of mourning. The new voice cannot replace the old ones and does not attempt to do so; no voice, no person, no aspect of one's life can replace another. But there can be a sense that the new voice has somehow been there all along in the old ones – as a child is somehow an immanence in his ancestors, and is brought to life both through their lives and through their deaths.
>
> *(Ogden, 2001, pp. 151–152)*

This unique concept of the work of mourning is based on the assumption that the process of mourning involves not only the ability to lament what was lost, but also the capacity to focus upon what might be born out of loss. The process of re-establishment of the lost object is based to a great extent on the ability to repeat the primary processes of internalization.

Melanie Klein, in her paper on mourning and its relation to manic-depressive states, points out that in the course of the normal work of mourning, the mourner repeats diachronically what he achieved in childhood (Klein, 1940). We may say that the more experienced a person is in developing processes of internalization, the easier it will be for him or her to deal with the work of mourning. I do not mean just the degree of internalization of the lost object itself, but the extent of the person's experience in processes of internalization in general. The more often and the more successfully one has made his way from the exterior to the interior, as well as from the actual to the possible – the easier it will be for him to cope with the transfer of the lost object from the exterior to the interior, with the belief and recognition that loss removes the object from the realm of the actual, but never from the realm of the possible (Gilead, 2003). The process of mourning locates the object within the psyche, and thereby protects it from further loss.

In his book *The Matrix of the Mind*, Thomas Ogden suggests that since in the paranoid-schizoid position there is no experience of historical continuity, and history is, in effect, re-written every moment, objects do not die, but disappear without a trace not only from the present and future but also from the past. From the paranoid-schizoid viewpoint, the concept of death is less absolute than from the depressive viewpoint, for there is always the possibility of an omnipotent re-creation of the missing object. Therefore, the work of mourning is a process of working out a depressive anxiety, and not a paranoid-schizoid anxiety (Ogden, 1986).

When there is no integration between the actual and the possible, the self must choose between concrete clinging to the actual object in order to maintain its continuous existence and psychotic clinging to the possible object in order to maintain it as an ever-becoming, emergent one. The first mechanism is found, for instance, in cases of obsessive love and obsessive harassment, as well as within imitative relationships in which the lover imitates the behaviour of the beloved, and even aspires to become him or her, as a sort of assurance of his own existence within the object and of the object's existence within himself. But most cases of obsessive love include alternation between these two possibilities: the obsessive lover obsessively clings to the object of his love, and through this clinging retains its actual continuity. Simultaneously, he projects his own possible dimension onto the actual dimension of the other in a way that does not take either the actual or the possible dimension of the other into account (as is to be expected in normal love relationships). The projection of his possible dimension onto the other creates a combination of obsessive concrete clinging to actual reality along with psychotic interpretations of this reality.

The work of mourning can undoubtedly be conceived of as a type of relationship, or as a model of object relationships. The more developed the self is, the more effectively will it express its ability to transfer the lost object from a state of actuality to a state of possibility, and to conduct a dialogue with it in a way which takes into account the object's possible dimension, rather than merely projecting onto it the self's own possible dimension. This will enable a deep process of growth within object relationship with the lost object and will strengthen the experience of defending this object against harm. In comparison with pathological expressions of mourning and melancholia, which attach themselves to the psychotic projection as a type of defense against reality – or alternatively become enslaved to this reality (and thereby lose the ability to maintain contact with anything beyond the actual) – this model proposes a process of working through which also involves the possibility of rehabilitation: a process whose borders are not those of memory, but those of imagination, and which involves the working through of relationships not only as they *were* but also as they *could have been* and therefore *could ever be*.

"That which is only living can only die", T.S. Eliot once wrote (1944, p. 7). The one who converses only with the actual will be silenced in the moment of actual loss. But the one who maintains a lyrical contact with the possible – he grasps eternity. This lyrical contact is what turns the absence of the actual into the possibility of eternity, or into an eternal possibility.

Notes

1 This chapter is based on the paper: Amir, D. (2008). Naming The Non-existent: Melancholia as Mourning Over a Possible Object. *The Psychoanalytic Review*, 95(1), pp. 1–15. Copyright: Guilford Press. Reprinted with permission of The Guilford Press.
2 I am using the terms "possible" and "actual" (Gilead, 1999, 2003) in the same sense that I used them while discussing Gilead's ideas in previous chapters (especially Chapter 3).
3 "There is no end to this love [. . .] and it can survive even the actual death of the loved one" (Gilead, 2003, p. 439).

References

Eliot, T.S. (1944). *Four Quartets*. London: Faber & Faber.

Freud, S. (1917). Mourning and Melancholia. In *The Standard Edition of the Complete Psychological Works of Sigmund Freud, Volume XIV (1914–1916): On the History of the Psycho-Analytic Movement, Papers on Metapsychology and Other Works*. London: The Hogarth Press, pp. 237–258.

Gilead, A. (1999). *Saving Possibilities: A Study in Philosophical Psychology*. Amsterdam: Rodopi.

Gilead, A. (2003). How Does Love Make the Ugly Beautiful? *Philosophy and Literature*, Vol. 27(2), pp. 436–443.

Klein, M. (1940). Mourning and its Relation to Manic-Depressive States. In *The Writings of Melanie Klein, Volume 1*, R. Money-Kyrle, B. Joseph, E. O'Shaughnessy, H. Segal, Eds. London: The Hogarth Press, 1975, pp. 344–369.

Ogden, T. (1986). *The Matrix of the Mind*. Northvale, NJ; London: Jason Aronson.

Ogden, T. (2001). Borges and the Art of Mourning. In *Conversations at the Frontier of Dreaming*. Northvale, NJ; London: Jason Aronson, pp. 115–152.

10

FROM THE EARTHLY JERUSALEM TO THE HEAVENLY CITY

The lyrical dimension of mourning in A.B. Yehoshua's novella *A Woman in Jerusalem*

The novella *A Woman in Jerusalem* is about a funeral procession, or rather about a process of mourning. This journey proceeds from outside in, from objective to subjective, and perhaps most of all from the actual to the possible, the two of which come together in the end. The novella's sub-title, "A Passion in Three Parts", tells us that what we have here is not a simple mission, but rather a story about desire, about revelation, perhaps even about fulfillment. Indeed, *the human resources person's journey* (which is the Hebrew title of this novella) is a journey that comes to restore the soul, aimed to infuse the capacity to yearn and to dream into an existence which has hitherto consisted of mere actions. It is a journey that restores subjectivity to a person who has existed until then as an object only.

Still, any reading of this story in terms solely of a person's relations to himself would, to an extent, miss its allegorical, symbolic dimension. For this journey does not just span between a person and himself but also between him and his place or God (in Hebrew the word *Ha'makom* refers both to a place and to the Talmudic God). It is no coincidence that the human resources manager's travel starts off in the earthly, divided Jerusalem, city of conflict and killings, and ends with the heavenly Jerusalem, the eternal city which can remain one and complete even when shared. The plot does not merely outline an individual psychic journey; it is, at the same time, a symbolical voyage whose lyrical conclusion touches on collective existence no less than on private lives.

The plot of the story concerns a non-Jewish woman in her forties who has immigrated to Israel from the former Soviet Union. She dies tragically in a terrorist attack on Jerusalem's vegetable market, and her corpse remains unidentified in the morgue. A search of her shopping bag reveals a pay slip, from which it transpires that she was employed as a cleaner in a large bakery in Jerusalem. In the bakery, however, no one has noted her absence. When the local paper publishes an item criticizing the owner of the bakery and his human resources manager for their inhuman and aloof attitude towards the dead employee, the owner of the bakery checks with the human resources person whether the woman had in fact been working for them, and if so, how it was possible that no one registered her absence. What begins as a series of uncomplicated bureaucratic actions, takes the human resources manager on a journey of self-discovery, cleansing and atonement. He finds himself accompanying the coffin of the dead woman – who somehow fascinates both her manager as well as many other people – for burial in her country of origin. This journey, which is nothing but a long drawn-out funeral procession, becomes a voyage into the manager's soul. While, at the outset of the novella we join the human resources manager on an exhaustingly detailed investigation of the concrete records of the factory, we gradually find ourselves, together with him and like him, drawn into the psyche's deepest archives.

Who is this human resources manager? A dull and inarticulate man with schizoid tendencies, whose orderly and concrete way of going about things has helped him ahead professionally, but has left his relations with his wife and one daughter sterile and empty. When we first meet him, we face a mass of details and the tiresome follow-up of facts, which he is unable to connect or make any sense of. A first hint at the possible existence of another psychic dimension is in the form of his inexplicable attraction to the dead woman's beauty – and the restlessness he feels when he hears her beauty mentioned by those who met her either before her death or after it. Can such beauty really have brushed so closely by me and have escaped my notice? – he wonders again and again. But why is he so troubled by this? Getting to see scores of people applying for jobs, every year, it should not really come as a surprise if he fails to recollect each and every one of them; especially a cleaner, a temporary job – one of those you never know whether they'll hold out beyond the trial period.

What is it, then, that keeps nagging at him? Here is where the foundations for what will eventually form the real plot emerge. It is not the dead woman's beauty that troubles the human resources manager's mind, or even her lonely, anonymous death. What tortures his soul is the fact that he could have stayed untouched by such beauty. This, he feels, is more telling about him than about her. Since the cleaner was not a young woman whose beauty would be easily recognizable to every eye (to the extent that beauty can ever be a matter of simple agreement), but a mother of an adolescent boy and in her forties – her type of beauty required a more contemplative or profound perspective in order to be noted. This is exactly the perspective that the human resources manager lacks. He is perturbed, therefore, not simply because he has failed to see her beauty, but because he has to confront the fact that he misses a psychic dimension. This is the dimension that is in charge of the ability to identify what is singular – both in others and in one's self; the dimension that is responsible for what I will call below "the beautiful".

It is the encounter with this that the human resources manager's meeting with the dead woman's beautiful son narrates. The beauty of this boy is such – suggests the reporter who accompanies the human resources manager on his journey – that it attracts women and men alike. We also learn that the boy has something of his mother: his eyes are stretched in the same unique "Tatar bow", the very feature of her that caught the eye of so many. This boy, we are told, is associated with "criminal elements". While their nature is never made explicit, later in the story it becomes clear that these words refer to a certain kind of physical relations which are "not innocent", and which leave bite marks on the boy's back. The human resources manager, who did not notice the mother's beauty, does not remain insensitive to her son's beauty and gradually falls for him.

What does the beauty of this boy as well as the human resources manager's attraction to him represent? Though there are clear suggestions of the erotic tension that the human resources manager tries very hard to fend off, the main revelation of this journey deep into himself is not homoerotic attraction. This novella is not about the actual, physical, concrete expressions of love – any type of love; it is about the very ability to love. The human resources manager is not attracted by beauty but by the beautiful, not by a beloved one but by love as such.

It is not by coincidence that he and the reporter – whom he calls "the weasel" – end up having a discussion about Plato's *Symposium* and the meaning of love:

> Human desire ascends by rungs like those of a ladder from love's lowest manifestations to its highest, from its most concrete to its most abstract, from its most physical to its most spiritual. To have the world of true form revealed to one is the reward of the wise lover – who, freed of the physical object of desire, realizes that his pursuit is of something more essential. The more he searches for it, the more he realizes that the ultimate beauty lies not in the body but in the soul [. . .] Love, says the weasel on behalf of Plato, reveals our finitude but also our ability to overcome that finitude.
>
> *(Yehoshua, 2006, pp. 156–157)*

And further on:

> "That's love's secret", the weasel continued as the vehicle slowed to take the hairpin bends. "There is no formula. Each person has to find the secret for himself. That's why Eros is neither god nor man. He's a *daimon*, thick-skinned, unwashed, barefoot, homeless, and poor – and he links the human to the divine, the temporal to the eternal . . ."
>
> *(Yehoshua, 2006, p. 157)*

The boy, a dirty homeless (the sour smell of his body is mentioned again and again), represents *eros*. While he is gentle, there is also a toughness about him – so that in the human resources manager's mind he comes to link between the divine and the human, being partially human, partially a demon (with "criminal elements"), partially an angel. The secret of love, explains the weasel, lies in the ability to perceive what is unique in both self and other, as well as in the interaction between them. It lies in the ability to see the other over and beyond his actual traits, thus folding the infinite into the knowledge of finitude. The human resources manager's attraction to the boy is, in a way, a yearning for a psychic revelation that will enable him to overcome the limitations of his concrete, temporal body, and gain eternal life.

Thus, he learns that the true desire for *the beautiful* is not the desire to conquer the object of love, but rather the desire to cross beyond the constraints of physical existence and pass into a higher sphere of being, to a kind of "heavenly Jerusalem". This is the desire to turn what depends on the body into something that transcends it; the desire to discover how the object of love is also present in other objects of love – much like Jerusalem has different manifestations beyond its physical location and its actual affinities. In this sense, indeed, Jerusalem does not belong to the human resources manager, or to the owner of the bakery, or to the reporter, or even to the deceased woman herself: it belongs to everyone.

Like Socrates' attitude in the *Symposium* towards young Alcibiades, the human resources manager does not reject the approaches of the deceased woman's son but nor does he respond to them. Instead he rises early and goes to the market square where he is tempted to have a bowl of hot soup. This gives him food poisoning, causing him to regress into a state of infantile helplessness through the total loss of sphincter control. One way of understanding this poisoning is as the human resources manager's bid to come clean of his sin.

But what, in fact, is his sin? Just before he begins eating the soup, he observes the baby of the cook who lies near the steaming pan. He thinks how he would like to approach the child and touch it. When he is surrounded by the peasant women, he says to himself: "But the baby is a lost cause. I can't play with it in front of all these anxious women" (p. 173). Could it be that the play he is forfeiting is not innocent but a sexual yearning? Such desires obviously lie somewhere buried in the depths of the human resources manager's psyche. But it would seem that much beyond sexual desire, this is about another desire: the desire for a psychic birth. And the only way for such a birth to occur is to absolutely surrender control of functional behaviour and of the orders of things, thus let himself go completely into the capricious rhythm of his needs; to give up on the objective adult and to gain, instead, the infant or the freedom to be a newborn.

The personal-psychic layer occludes another layer: this is not merely about the human resources manager's wish to be reborn as a feeling, desiring and dreaming subject, but also about the birth of the ability to see beyond the actual facts, to transform one's experience from two to three-dimensional, to substitute the struggle for a concrete place with one for psychic space. For this to happen, A.B. Yehoshua teaches us, one has to become cleansed of concrete vision, of material yearnings and bodily needs, and to rise to a higher level of vision and existence, a level on which ownership is not determined by staking out the actual boundaries of what owned but on the basis of its internalization, that is: its situation within one's psychic world.

The human resources manager's voyage into himself, into his heavenly Jerusalem, turns him from possessing a civil servant's judgement to having inner awareness; from being an owner of documents to being an owner of dreams. The constitution of interiority enables the human resources manager not only to love but also to mourn. As suggested before, the process of working through mourning essentially depends on the ability to transform the lost object from an actual into a possible one. The human resources manager's voyage is indeed a voyage from the actual to the possible: from an attempt to reconstruct the actual figure of the deceased woman to one that builds her possible figure and on that basis engages in a living and breathing dialogue with her; from the decision to make amends for sin by concrete means to the insight that true atonement does not lie in restoring reality but rather in the reconstitution of the dream.

There is, hence, a good reason for the fact that this journey – in the course of which the human resources manager renounces his objective criteria, logic, the sense of time and control – ends with a lyrical solution. The deceased woman's mother tells them to take her daughter's coffin back to Israel and to bury her in the city in which she chose to live, and which belongs to her as it does to everybody else. Earlier on, when he addresses the people of the woman's village, the human resources manager says:

> As for me, I am not a messenger who comes and goes. I am a human resources manager whose duty it is to remain with you until the last clod of earth has fallen on my employee's grave, before returning to the city which is for me only a bitter reality.
>
> *(Yehoshua, 2006, p. 191)*

In this sentence inheres the secret that forms the entire point of this voyage. For the same Jerusalem, which to him is nothing but a bitter reality, was the dream of Julia Ragayev, the absentee heroine of this novella. What symbolized the actual for him, stood for the possible for her. Jerusalem did indeed belong to her like to everybody else, even though she was a stranger, because what she had in mind was not the earthly Jerusalem, city of conflict and killings, but the heavenly Jerusalem: city of dreams, of hopes; a city which for each and every human represents the eternal. Her mother was right to tell the human resources manager to change the direction of his journey and to take her daughter back from the lower lands to the high ground, from the actual to the possible, from the sphere of reality to that of the dream.

"That's just it", the human resources manager says to the bakery owner in their final conversation, "We've got to the painful part, but not to the end" (p. 196). The journey that this novella describes stretches, indeed, not from beginning to end or from birth to death: it moves from the outside in. It proceeds from the actual facts into the core and essence of things. And since its boundaries are not those of the actual but those of the possible – not the things as they were, but as they might have been – this lyrical journey concludes, rather than with the act of atonement itself, with the understanding that in the realm of the possible one can repair even what actually no longer exists and can no longer be repaired.

The human resources manager's journey is not a lament for Julia Ragayev but a struggle for the creation of a new voice out of her loss. It is the recognition of the loss of the actual object that allows him to find the possible one. Recognizing what she was and will no longer be enables him the recognition of what she could have been and henceforth will forever be. It is therefore not surprising that this profound journey ends not at the threshold of reality but on the frontier of dream. A.B. Yehoshua redirects both his readers and his hero to Jerusalem, which until that point was no more than a bitter reality, so that they will transform it from a place down below into the elevated psychic space that will allow it and them eternal life.

Reference

Yehoshua, A.B. (2006). *A Woman in Jerusalem*, trans. Hilel Halkin. London: Halban.

11

ON LYRICISM, KNOWLEDGE AND LOVE

In a beautiful chapter dedicated to the nature of esthetic judgement, the psychoanalyst Donald Meltzer and the literary scholar Meg Harris-Williams consider the way in which the individual psyche adjusts itself to the esthetic object. In the encounter between self and object, they argue, two modes of contact are exposed: *carving* and *enveloping*. It is between these modes of contact that the drama of the inner world finds its symbolic form. The foundation from which the psyche emerges is the interaction between the infant's psyche and the mother-world's bodily spaces. On this basis all developmental thought processes evolve as well as the "essential knowing", above and beyond "knowing about" (1988, pp. 186–187).

What are the functions of carving and enveloping?

In my belief, carving and enveloping are not just two functions that characterize the encounter between self and object or between self and esthetic object, but expressions of the two constitutive functions of the self as such: the emergent self, which can be conceived as the aspect that is responsible for carving, for revelation and singularity, and the continuous self, which can be seen as the aspect in charge of enveloping, that is, of containing what is carved between the firm walls of continuity, causality and memory. This encounter between carving and enveloping, or between the emergent that unveils the world in all its singularity and the continuous that embraces that singularity in the context of continuous being, is the foundation from which Meltzer and Harris-Williams suggest essential knowing evolves. This foundation, I believe, is the lyrical dimension.

How does the lyrical dimension of the psyche serve as the groundwork of the above two types of knowing? And what, in fact, is the difference between "essential knowing" and "knowing-about"?

While "knowing-about" is a form of knowing that relates to the object from an external point of view, from a distance, as it attempts to envelop and subsume the new and singular within the existing order of the familiar, "essential knowing" concerns knowing the new in itself. This latter form of knowing aims to reveal, release and penetrate the core and essence of things. In our present terms we can consider "knowing-about" as knowing the *actual object*, while essential knowing can be regarded as knowing the *possible object* (Gilead, 1999).

Amihud Gilead, in his paper "How Does Love Make the Ugly Beautiful?" writes: "to love means to reveal, to create or discover beauty" (Gilead, 2003, p. 436). According to him, beauty is not merely in the eye of the beholder, but also waits to be revealed. Much like sculptors who must reveal and disclose the sculpture hidden in the marble – beauty is often hidden under layers of apparent plainness, waiting for the lover, artist or poet in order to be uncovered. What Gilead means is not the well-known cliché that a physically unattractive person may well have a beautiful soul and hence arouse love, but rather that love brings out, even from behaviours and traits that under different circumstances would seem annoying or ridiculous, the shrouded and singular meaning they carry within. When we fail to love a person, we also remain blind to the deep significance and meaning of his physical properties by not perceiving them as features that harbour beauty.

"Physical beauty is only an actualization of mental beauty, as much as anything actual is only an actualization of its possibility, which is also its identity", argues Gilead. "Under the identity of something, we may conceive not only its actual being and states but also all the possibilities of change or variation, in the range of which it still keeps its own identity" (Gilead, 2003, p. 436). "The art of love, therefore, makes the physically ugly beautiful by means of revealing its hidden meanings and significance" (*ibid.*, pp. 442–443).

When we consider love as a form of knowing, we have in mind not only the lover's knowing of the beloved. It is knowing in itself that we refer to: the kind of knowing that may address itself equally to an idea, a thing or a person.

What, then, is the role of the lyrical dimension in the human ability to know?

Since the carving function within the process of knowing depends on the emergent self, while the function of enveloping depends on the continuous self, the mutual adjustment between carving and enveloping – or, alternatively, the nature of the interaction between the carving function and the enveloping function while encountering a new subject matter – is determined by the quality of interaction between the emergent self and the continuous self, and, hence, by the quality of the lyrical dimension.

The carving–enveloping interaction is also closely linked with the relationship between the actual and the possible. Expanding on Gilead's claim (1999, 2003) that the possible comes prior to and is broader than the actual, thus including and encompassing it, I suggest that the actual is not merely the partial realization of the possible, but may as well serve as a limit and an envelope allowing for the psychic motion towards that possible. Carving is not possible without enveloping, and so the possible can only be carved when it is enveloped and protected by the boundaries of the actual. I would like to emphasize that there is no contradiction whatsoever between this claim and the claim that the possible antecedes the actual. The actual, indeed, derives from the possible and constitutes a partial realization of the a priori reservoir that each person carries within.

Psychic birth, however, does not come to an end with one single transformation of the possible to the actual, at the very beginning of the individual's life, determining his or her identity from then on. It is rather a dynamic process which lasts through a person's lifetime. That is, while the act of birth is directed from the possible to the actual, the direction of development throughout life is from the actual to the possible. Psychic development, as well as the processes of knowing and loving, is grounded in the attempt to identify and extract the possible from the actual.

Whenever we encounter the possible we enrich our psychic existence, or its actual dimensions, with an additional dimension. The possible is not just the reason for our existence as we are, but also the aim towards which this existence strains by its very essence. The entire psychic motion as such is propelled by that striving to make contact with the a priori possible. The contact with the possible, however, cannot occur other than as part of our actual existence, for each time such a contact takes place it constitutes an actualization. In other words: while the possible exists independently of the actual and precedes it, the contact with the possible can only occur in the context of the actual existence. For love to extract the possible beauty from the constraints of the beloved's actual one – a lover is needed, as well as a loved one and the actualization of love.

Between a person's birth (the transition from possible to actual) and his death (the absolute passage from actual to possible), spans a whole life consisting of a reciprocal and continuous motion between the possible and the actual. The lyrical dimension does not only serve as the unique arbitrator for that part of the possible that will become actual at the onset of a person's life, but goes on directing him or her in maintaining contact with one's own possible dimension as well as with the possible dimension of the other. Each moment when such contact between a person's actual existence and his or her possible dimension occurs, the possible undergoes actualization in the sense of becoming manifest as a part of that person's psyche. But the possible that does not become fully actualized also exists throughout in the form of inner lining or an additional dimension which bestows actual existence with depth and resonance, a horizon to which the psyche orients itself for ever.

As mentioned earlier, we can distinguish between two modes or two levels of knowing. The lower level is that of "knowing-about", while the higher or more evolved one is that of "essential knowing". While the first level of knowing addresses itself to the actual object, the second aims at the possible one. Every process of knowing, as said, is based on a certain interaction or interrelation between carving and enveloping, between emergent and continuous, between the desire, on one hand, to reveal what is *sui generis* in things and, on the other, to "wrap" this singularity in a familiar context that enables us to situate it on a historical, logical and emotional continuum.

Of these two levels of knowing, knowing-about relies more on the function of enveloping than on the function of carving. Here the continuous dominates the emergent so that the process of knowing is directed at recognizing the familiar within the new: putting the new object in a familiar frame rather than touching on its unknown, foreign, singular aspects which cannot be captured either by reference to a logical or emotional order, or as a part of historical experience. Essential knowing, by contrast, is grounded in the carving rather than in the enveloping function. At this level of knowing, the emergent dominates over the continuous so that the function of knowing is entirely directed at the unveiling of the object's new, unique, singular and unfamiliar aspects. While knowing-about is directed at *what is*, that is, at the actual – essential knowing aims at *what may be*, that is, at the possible. And while knowing-about is driven by the wish to recognize the object as it is – essential knowing is motivated by the longing to identify what the object holds within as a possibility.

As said above, we are not dealing merely with knowing in the emotional sense, the kind of knowing that touches another person and occurs in the context of our connection with any other, but with a type of knowing that relates to our inner link with any idea or thought. One can easily tell the difference between someone who is connected to a certain field of knowledge yet remains separate from it – and someone who is so profoundly tied to that field of knowledge that he seems to know it from within. We can intuitively distinguish between mathematicians who have an intuitive grasp of the solution and mathematicians who take a linear course towards it; between physicians who look at their patient and intuitively understand the source of his pains and those who only manage to do so after consulting an X-ray; between musicians who sense the music and those who digitally "read" their scores but do not have an inner experience of the counterpoint. The distinction, in all these cases, is between knowing-about and essential knowing, or between the tendency to look for a solution that follows in a direct line from existing knowledge and the tendency to discover a new solution, one that does not emerge from a natural continuation of already accumulated knowledge but constitutes a kind of quantum leap, maybe even a kind of "Kefitzat-Haderech".

Essential knowing is the psychic state which is perhaps the closest to love. It is the deepest and most intuitive form of knowing and of the two modes of knowing discussed here it represents the more natural connection to the thing in itself.[1] Knowing here is of the thing from within oneself, not only from within itself. This mode of knowing is not only a process through which one "penetrates" an object of knowledge and deciphers its internal code, but also an encounter in which one allows that object to penetrate and decode one's own interiority. In this sense, this is an interactive, inter-subjective reciprocal process of knowing, a kind of knowing that is not static (as is knowing-about) but dynamic, alive and subject to constant change.

This is the knowledge of the possible, which by definition lacks clear boundaries, and is dynamic and ambiguous. And since knowing always carries some of its subject's features – we may say that much like the possible is more extensive than the actual and precedes it, so essential knowing is more extensive than knowing-about. Exactly as the actual constitutes the limit that allows us to maintain the link with the possible, so knowing-about exists as the limit that contains and enables essential knowing. Essential knowing without knowing-about could be extremely haphazard and dangerous. By contrast – knowing-about, devoid of essential knowing – will most likely be barren and meaningless. We therefore return to the issue of the integration between these two forms of knowing. While I agree with Meltzer and Harris-Williams that essential knowing ranks higher in the hierarchy of knowing than knowing-about, I argue that both levels require each other in order to exist and actually entertain a dialectic relationship in which the existence of the one validates and renders significant the existence of the other.

There is a reason why this journey into human lyricism concludes with a statement about love. Love itself is based on the dialectic between these two types of knowing. Our capacity to love the possible in our significant ones not only transcends their actual limits but is also contained in and protected by them. The lyrical balance between knowing the actual object and knowing the possible one not only constitutes the foundation for our ability to know the other, any other – but is also the profoundest secret concerning our ability to love that other, both outside and within ourselves.

Note

1 These ideas reflect in a way Spinoza's three degrees of knowledge and the relationship between the highest degree, that of the intellectual love of God, and the other degrees of consciousness and their emotional qualities.

References

Gilead, A. (1999). *Saving Possibilities: A Study in Philosophical Psychology*. Amsterdam: Rodopi.
Gilead, A. (2003). How Does Love Make the Ugly Beautiful? *Philosophy and Literature*, 27(2), pp. 436–443.
Meltzer, D. and Harris-Williams, M. (1988). Holding the Dream. In *The Apprehension of Beauty*. Scotland: Clunie Press, pp. 178–199.

INDEX